Peter Malin

Series Editor: Marian Cox

The Winter's Tale

William Shakespeare

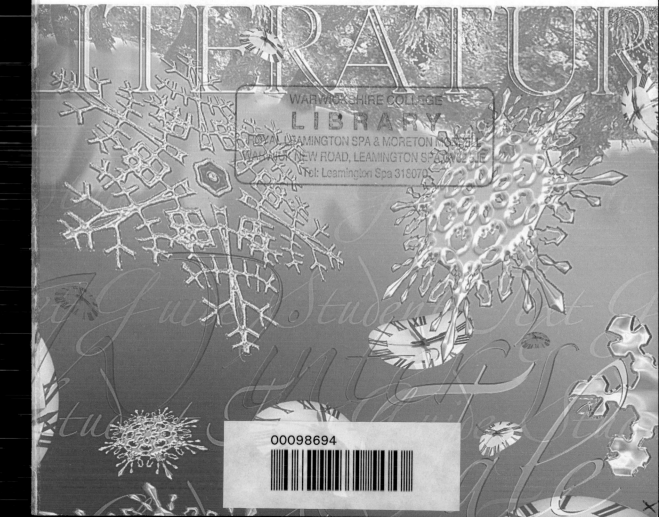

Philip Allan Updates
Market Place
Deddington
Oxfordshire
OX15 0SE
Tel: 01869 338652
Fax: 01869 337590
e-mail: sales@philipallan.co.uk
www.philipallan.co.uk

ISBN-13: 978-1-84489-401-7
ISBN-10: 1-84489-401-0

Printed by MPG Books, Bodmin

Environmental information
The paper on which this title is printed is sourced from mills using wood from managed, sustainable forests.

Contents

Introduction

Aims of the guide

The purpose of this Student Text Guide to *The Winter's Tale* is to support your study of the play, whether you are approaching it as an examination text or for coursework. It is not a substitute for your own reading, rereading, thinking and note-making about the text. The ideas about the play contained in this guide are based on the interpretation of one reader. What the examiners want is your own considered response, and they can easily recognise an answer that simply repeats a critical viewpoint at second hand. As you use this guide, you should be constantly questioning what it says; you may find yourself disagreeing with some of the analysis, which in itself could form an interesting starting-point for your own interpretative view.

Quotations and line references in this guide refer to the Cambridge School Shakespeare edition of *The Winter's Tale*, edited by Sheila Innes and Elizabeth Huddlestone (Cambridge University Press, 1999). If you are using another edition, the references should be easy enough to find, though there will inevitably be a few lines' difference in scenes containing prose. References to other plays by Shakespeare are to the Oxford *Complete Works*, compact edition, edited by Stanley Wells and Gary Taylor (Clarendon Press, 1988). In referring to modern performances of the play, the initials RSC stand for the Royal Shakespeare Company. Dates given refer to the year in which a particular production opened.

The remainder of this Introduction outlines the principal exam board Assessment Objectives, and offers advice on revision and how to approach both coursework and exam essays. I am indebted to the series editor, Marian Cox, whose own Student Text Guides I have used in composing this introductory section.

The Text Guidance section consists of a series of subsections which examine key aspects of the play. These include contexts; a scene-by-scene commentary on the play; analysis of characters, language and themes; the play's critical and theatrical afterlife; useful quotations; and a selected glossary of literary terms.

The final section, Questions and Answers, includes suggested essay questions, sample essay plans with marking guidelines, and a series of exemplar essays.

Exam board specifications

The Winter's Tale features on a number of exam specifications for either AS or A2. It is also possible to study the play for coursework, either by itself or in comparison with another text.

It is important that you scrutinise the particular specification you are following. This will indicate not just where the play fits into the context of the whole subject, but such practical matters as the format and style of exam questions, how long you have to answer them, and whether you are allowed to have your copy of the text in the exam room with you. Most importantly, the specification makes clear which of the Assessment Objectives are tested through your response to this particular text, and what their relative weighting is. This is just as important if you are producing a coursework essay on the play.

Assessment Objectives

The Assessment Objectives (AOs) for AS and A2 English Literature are common to all boards:

AO1	communicate clearly the knowledge, understanding and insight appropriate to literary study, using appropriate terminology and accurate and coherent written expression
AO2i	respond with knowledge and understanding to literary texts of different types and periods
AO2ii	respond with knowledge and understanding to literary texts of different types and periods, exploring and commenting on relationships and comparisons between literary texts
AO3	show detailed understanding of the ways in which writers' choices of form, structure and language shape meanings
AO4	articulate independent opinions and judgements, informed by different interpretations of literary texts by other readers
AO5i	show understanding of the contexts in which literary texts are written and understood
AO5ii	evaluate the significance of cultural, historical and other contextual influences on literary texts and study

A summary and paraphrase of each Assessment Objective is given below and would be worth memorising:

AO1	clarity of written communication
AO2	informed personal response in relation to time and genre (literary context)
AO3	the creative literary process (context of writing)
AO4	critical and interpretative response (context of reading)
AO5	evaluation of influences (cultural context)

It is essential that you pay close attention to the AOs and their weightings for the board for which you are entered: your teacher will be able to give you this information. For example, in AQA Specification A, the dominant AO on *The Winter's Tale* is AO4; hence you would need to concentrate on demonstrating an awareness of differing interpretations of the text. Once you have identified the relevant AOs and their weightings, you must address them explicitly in your answer, in addition to showing your overall familiarity with and understanding of the text and demonstrating your ability to offer a clear, relevant and convincing argument.

Coursework

You will probably be able to choose your own focus for coursework, but it is vital that the topic you choose enables you to meet the relevant Assessment Objectives. For a comparative essay, you need to check if you are required to compare the play with any particular genre of text, e.g. a novel, or a play from another period. You then need to choose a text that has obvious points of comparison and contrast, for example one that deals with the issue of jealousy, or works through tragic events to reach a positive resolution, or mixes comic and serious scenes and characters, or uses powerful imagery of nature and the seasons.

You may be allowed to present a creative response to the text as your coursework assignment. This should be accompanied by an explanation of the rationale behind your approach and an account of how it relates to the text.

Although handwritten essays may be permissible, it is far better to word process your coursework. Not only will this make your own process of composition and redrafting easier, but it also shows consideration for your teachers and for coursework moderators, who have a large number of lengthy essays to read and assess. Double line spacing will also help them to annotate your work.

From the moment you begin planning your essay, you need to be aware of how long it is expected to be. Essays that diverge radically from the word limit, in either direction, are penalised. Again, using a computer enables you to keep a regular check on the number of words you have written.

Approaching a coursework essay

You should be given a reasonable period of time to produce your essay. Don't assume that this means you can relax. If you have three weeks to complete your essay, do not leave it to the middle of the third week before you begin. After all, if you were writing a 45-minute exam essay, you would not sit doing nothing for the first 35 minutes. There are a number of key stages in the coursework writing process:

- Choose your title and discuss it with your teacher as soon as possible.
- Make sure you know what the examiners expect from a coursework essay for the specification you are following. Always focus on the Assessment Objectives that are

actually being tested through the coursework unit — ask your teacher to make sure.

- Reread the play and all the notes and essays you have already written on it, extract what is relevant and start to allow ideas to develop in your mind.
- Set aside an hour to jot down ideas for the essay and convert them into an essay plan. Share this plan with your teacher and make use of any feedback offered.
- Identify any background reading, such as textual criticism, that may be useful to you, gather the books you need, read them and make notes.
- Give yourself a reasonable period to draft the essay, working with your text, your notes and other useful materials around you.
- Keep referring back to the title or question, and make sure that you remain focused on it.
- Allow time for your teacher to read and comment on at least part of your draft.
- Redraft your essay until you are satisfied with it. Keep checking that you have focused on the relevant Assessment Objectives.
- Leave plenty of time to complete your final version. Don't just copy it up from your draft — be prepared to add and edit, rephrase and polish.
- A bibliography will add to the professionalism of your essay. This should list all the texts you have quoted from and consulted. Check with your teacher whether you are required to use any particular format for a bibliography, and do not deviate from it.
- Proofread your essay carefully before handing it in.

Examinations

Revision advice

For the examined units it is possible that either brief or extensive revision will be necessary because the original study of the text took place some time previously. It is therefore useful to know how to go about revising and which tried and tested methods are considered the most successful for literature exams at all levels, from GCSE to degree finals. There are no short-cuts to effective exam revision; the only way to know a text well, and to know your way around it in an exam, is to have done the necessary studying. If you use the following method for both open and closed book revision, you will not only revisit and reassess all your previous work on the text in a manageable way but be able to distil, organise and retain your knowledge. Don't try to do it all in one go: take regular breaks for refreshment and a change of scene.

(1) Between a month and a fortnight before the exam, depending on your schedule (a simple list of stages with dates displayed in your room, not a work of art), you will need to reread the text, this time taking stock of all the underlinings and marginal annotations as well. As you read, collect onto sheets of A4 the essential

ideas and quotations as you come across them. The acts of selecting key material and recording it as notes are natural ways of stimulating thought and aiding memory.

(2) Reread the highlighted areas and marginal annotations in your critical extracts and background handouts, and add anything useful from them to your list of notes and quotations. Then reread your previous essays and the teachers' comments. As you look back through essays written earlier in the course, you should have the pleasant sensation of realising that you can now write much better on the text than you could then. You will also discover that much of your huge file of notes is redundant or repeated, and that you have changed your mind about some beliefs, so that the distillation process is not too daunting. Selecting what is important is the way to crystallise your knowledge and understanding.

(3) During the run-up to the exam you need to do lots of practice essay plans to help you identify any gaps in your knowledge and give you practice in planning in five to eight minutes. Past paper titles for you to plan are provided in this guide, some of which can be done as full timed essays — and marked strictly according to exam criteria — which will show whether length and timing are problematic for you. If you have not seen a copy of a real exam paper before you take your first module, ask to see a past paper so that you are familiar with the layout and rubric.

(4) About a week before the exam, reduce your two or three sides of A4 notes to a double-sided postcard of very small dense writing. Collect a group of key words by once again selecting and condensing, and use abbreviations for quotations (first and last word), and character and place names (initials). The act of choosing and writing out the short quotations will help you to focus on the essential issues, and to recall them quickly in the exam. Make sure that your selection covers the main themes and includes examples of symbolism, style, comments on character, examples of irony, point of view or other significant aspects of the text. Previous class discussion and essay writing will have indicated which quotations are useful for almost any title; pick those which can serve more than one purpose, for instance those which reveal character and theme, and are also an example of language. In this way a minimum number of quotations can have maximum application.

(5) You now have in a compact, accessible form all the material for any possible essay title. There are only half a dozen themes relevant to a literary text so if you have covered these you should not meet with any nasty surprises when you read the exam questions. You do not need to refer to your file of paperwork again, or even to the text. For the few days before the exam, you can read through your handy postcard whenever and wherever you get the opportunity. Each time you read it, which will only take a few minutes, you will be reminding yourself of all the information you will be able to recall in the exam to adapt to the general title or to support an analysis of particular passages.

(6) A fresh, active mind works wonders, and information needs time to settle, so don't try to cram just before the exam. Relax the night before and get a good night's sleep. In this way you will be able to enter the exam room feeling the confidence of the well-prepared candidate.

Approaching an exam essay

Your precise approach to writing an essay in exam conditions will depend on how long you have to write it, the Assessment Objectives that are being tested, and whether you are allowed to have your copy of the text with you in the exam.

Choosing a question

- Choose carefully from any options available.
- The apparently 'easier' choice will not necessarily show you at your best: you might be tempted just to reproduce stale ideas without much thought.
- A question that looks more challenging may well result in much greater engagement with the issues and argument as you write.
- However, you must choose a question that you can approach with confidence.

Planning

- Identify and highlight the key words in the question. As you write the essay, keep checking back to ensure that you are dealing with these.
- If the question requires you to focus on a particular passage, either in your own text or printed on the exam paper, read through the passage, making brief annotations as you do so. You should know the text well enough not to be baffled by anything the set section contains.
- Brainstorm your ideas on your answer sheet. This should take no more than three or four minutes.
- Plan your essay. You will not have time to create a formal and detailed plan, but you should at least highlight on your brainstormed notes a rational order in which to deal with the points you have identified.
- If the question is in parts, either implicitly or explicitly, make sure you give equal attention to each separate requirement.
- Jot down the characters, themes, scenes, speeches, images etc. that might be useful to refer to in each part of your essay.

Writing

- Write your introductory paragraph. This might briefly set the context, define the question's key words, and give some indication of your line of approach. Sometimes, though, it is better to plunge straight into your analysis without any introductory waffling.
- Keep your mind partly on the quality of your own writing: think about sentence structures, paragraphing, vocabulary choices and use of appropriate technical

terms. Remember those useful words and phrases for moving on to a new point or changing direction: 'However', 'On the other hand', 'Alternatively', 'Nevertheless', 'Even so', 'In addition' etc. These can be useful paragraph starters.

- Write the rest of the essay. Keep checking back to the key words and cross off each point on your notes/plan as you have dealt with it. Check the time at regular intervals.
- Incorporate short, relevant quotations into your argument, weaving them into the grammatical structure of your own sentences. Make the point of longer quotations clear — don't expect them to speak for themselves.
- Create a brief concluding paragraph that gives an overview of your argument without simply repeating or summarising the points you have made. Your conclusion should sound conclusive even if it does not strongly support a particular interpretation.
- Check through what you have written, looking at both content and accuracy, and make neat corrections where necessary. You may wish to add brief points, using omission marks or asterisks, but do not be tempted to undertake any major alterations.
- Cross out your notes and planning with a neat diagonal line.

Further points

The exam paper is designed to test your ability to structure an argument around the specific issues in a question. You must not simply use the question as a peg on which to hang an essay you are determined to write. If a question or title crops up that you have tackled before, don't just regurgitate your previous essay, but try to think about the issues from a fresh perspective.

Essay questions are usually open ended. Don't assume that you are expected to find a 'right answer'; instead, you need to demonstrate the ability to look at the issue from various angles, and perhaps to reach a qualified conclusion. You should certainly not offer a dismissive, extreme or entirely one-sided response. If you do have strong views of your own, and can argue them convincingly, this is evidence of an informed personal response, but you still need to show an awareness of alternative interpretations. You will learn a great deal about what the examiners are looking for by studying:

- the published details of the subject specification
- the Assessment Objectives being tested in each particular part of the exam
- past exam papers
- the examiners' reports on the previous year's exams

Ask your teacher to go through the relevant parts of these documents with you.

Text Guidance

Contexts

Historical and cultural context

In common with any other culture, the Elizabethan and Jacobean age was racked by theological, political and social anxieties which inevitably colour the literature and drama of the time. In his commendatory verse published in the First Folio of Shakespeare's plays in 1623, his fellow dramatist Ben Jonson said of Shakespeare, 'He was not of an age, but for all time'. Readers, audiences and practitioners have often used Jonson's comment to promote Shakespeare's universality, in particular his sympathetic understanding of human nature, and we continue to concentrate in his plays on what we find relevant to our own experience of life and society at the expense of those elements that mark his work as specifically a product of English Renaissance culture. We can gain as much, though, from a consideration of what seems alien to us in his plays, as from responding to those ideas we can recognise and share. The following notes offer a brief introduction to some specific features of life in Jacobean England that relate to *The Winter's Tale*.

Queen Elizabeth and King James

The supreme power of the monarch as head of state was increasingly subject to critical scrutiny as the Tudor age, culminating in the long reign of Elizabeth I, gave way to that of her Stuart successor, James I. Maintaining the political status quo depended on numerous factors, not the least of which was ensuring a clear and strong line of succession. Since Elizabeth was unmarried and childless, anxieties about who would succeed her became acute as she moved into old age and ill health. Two years before Elizabeth's death, her former favourite, the Earl of Essex, had been executed after mounting an abortive rebellion against her, but Elizabeth stead-fastly refused to name an heir, stating that God would take care of England.

We can see these anxieties explored quite openly in the play: in many ways the most shocking element in the oracle's pronouncement is that 'the king shall live without an heir, if that which is lost be not found'. The horrible significance of this statement is evidently lost on the lords, who respond 'Now blessèd be the great Apollo!', and even on Hermione, who can only add 'Praised!' (III.2.134). Only when the servant enters to announce Mamillius's death does the actual meaning of the oracle hit home. The play's opening scene had made much of the prince's future potential, ending with the comment 'If the king had no son they would desire to live on crutches till he had one' (I.1.37–38), and in Act I scene 2 it was clear that both Polixenes and Leontes found in their respective sons the chief source of their content-ment. When Polixenes later threatens to disinherit Florizel — 'we'll bar thee from succession' (IV.4.408) — it creates a much more profound shock than may be apparent to us, and by Act V the question of succession is central to the political anxieties of the Sicilian lords as they urge Leontes to remarry. The kingdom is 'heirless' (V.1.10) and Leontes 'issueless' (V.1.173), and his stubbornness, supported by Paulina, is a source of intense frustration for his ministers.

During the last years of Elizabeth's reign, some of her courtiers had conducted secret correspondence with her cousin James VI of Scotland, whose mother, Mary, Queen of Scots, Elizabeth had had executed. When the queen died in March 1603, James succeeded peacefully to the English throne; whether she formally acknowledged him as heir on her deathbed is disputed. Paulina's statement that 'the crown will find an heir' echoes the attitude taken by Elizabeth, and when she talks of Alexander the Great leaving his crown to 'th'worthiest; so his successor | Was like to be the best' (V.1.47–49), this might be read by the Jacobean audience as a flattering comment addressed to King James, similar to those Shakespeare had scattered through the text of *Macbeth* just a few years earlier. When Hermione claims in the final scene that she has preserved herself to see 'the issue', she may primarily mean the outcome of events, but the noun is also overlaid with the senses of both 'child' and 'heir', as used so often elsewhere in the play.

In November 1612, life eerily imitated art when Prince Henry, the heir to the English crown, died in mysterious circumstances, probably of typhoid. Although he was not a child, like Mamillius, but a young man, and although James I had two other children to take up the royal succession, there must have been something of a *frisson* when the play was revived at court shortly after the prince's death. He and his father had conflicting political ideas, and there were rumours that the king had had a hand in his death, just as, in the play, Leontes is indirectly responsible for that of Mamillius.

The Jacobean court

Prince Henry's uneasy relationship with his father is reflected in the play by that of Florizel and Polixenes, too. At the time of his death, Henry's possible marriage was being negotiated with three foreign princesses, and the prince had made it clear that, whatever his own feelings, he was in the power of his father's decision on the subject. To engage in a romantic affair of his own, as Florizel does, and not merely with a commoner but a shepherdess, would have been unthinkable. In the play it is clear that he is taking a very dangerous course, and Polixenes's fury can only be fully understood in the political context of the time.

In view of the cordial relations between Sicilia and Bohemia, if Leontes's jealousy had not destroyed his family, the prospect of marriage between his daughter and Florizel would have been a likely political alliance. In another historical coincidence, one of Europe's most powerful and influential princes, the Elector Palatine, who married James I's daughter, Elizabeth, in 1613, became King of Bohemia six years later; *The Winter's Tale* had been one of 14 plays performed at court in

the two months of celebrations before their wedding, and its Bohemian setting would have acquired a particular resonance when it was played there again around 1618 or 1619.

Two months of pre-wedding celebrations in the context of international diplomacy may fall short of the nine-month visit of Polixenes to Sicilia that opens the play, but it gives an indication of the scale and duration of such elaborate diplomatic hospitality. James I was notorious for the extravagance of his court, and audiences at the Globe and Blackfriars would be well aware of the 'magnificence', to use Archidamus's word (I.1.10), of courtly entertainments. As well as plays, these would include the newly-popular genre of masques, which employed poetry, music, dance, scenery and spectacular effects in the service of political or moral allegories. There are masque-like elements in all of Shakespeare's final plays, and the statue scene in *The Winter's Tale* is one such, though the sheep-shearing festivities rival it in sheer stage spectacle. The satyr-dance performed by 'four threes of herdsmen' (IV.4.314–15) may well have been 'borrowed' from Ben Jonson's *Masque of Oberon*, which had been performed for James I on New Year's Day, 1611; hence, perhaps, the servant's assertion that 'one three of them [...] hath danced before the king' (IV.4.316–17).

Conspiracy and witchcraft

While expensive entertaining was one side of Jacobean court life, there were also more sinister and dangerous undercurrents. The Gunpowder Plot of 1605 was only one of a number of conspiracies mounted against James I and members of his government, and the influence of witchcraft was often evoked to demonise those suspected of involvement. Before succeeding to the English crown, King James himself had published a book on witchcraft entitled *Demonology*. The sensitivity of the subject, most notably evident in *Macbeth*, is reflected here in passing references such as Leontes's denigration of Paulina as 'a mankind witch' (II.3.67), Polixenes's ambivalent description of Perdita as a 'fresh piece | Of excellent witchcraft' (IV.4.401–02), and Paulina's anxiety at the end of the play that her animation of Hermione's statue should not be interpreted as 'unlawful business' (V.3.96) in which she is 'assisted | By wicked powers' (V.3.90–91). Leontes's assertion that 'There is a plot against my life, my crown' (II.1.47) may seem like a manifestation of his paranoia, but would have been recognised as the kind of genuine concern that gave real monarchs sleepless nights.

To counteract such conspiracies and rebellions, Renaissance courts employed sophisticated networks of spies, informers and hit-men, who could often, of course, be playing one side off against the other. Leontes expects Camillo to poison Polixenes as a matter of course, because he commands it. His automatic assumption when he fails to do so is that he was a double agent all along: 'That false villain | Whom I employed was pre-employed by him' (II.1.48–49); consequently, Polixenes is now safely back in Bohemia, 'plot-proof' (II.3.6). It is clear later that Polixenes's own court operates according to the same devious and covert methods, when he tells Camillo of the reports his spies, or intelligencers, have provided about Florizel's activities: 'I have eyes under my service which look upon his removedness' (IV.2.28–29) — something Camillo later refers back to when he says to Perdita, 'I do fear eyes over' (IV.4.623). Such activities were a necessary part of the maintenance of state security, and in view of the political differences between King James and the ill-fated Prince Henry, it is inevitable that the spying of father on son was a historical reality as much as a feature of Shakespeare's dramatic fiction.

Social class

Attitudes to social class in Shakespeare's time seem somewhat contradictory. There was still an assumption that character and social status went hand in hand, so that only aristocrats could demonstrate true nobility, even though this notion had been challenged at least as far back as Chaucer's 'The Wife of Bath's Tale'. Shakespeare's view seems notably ambivalent: ultimately, Perdita is a fit wife for Florizel only because she is in reality a princess; yet in his portrayal of the Shepherd and Clown Shakespeare makes it clear that human decency, charity and compassion are not qualities confined to the gentry. The play rewards them by their comic elevation to being 'gentlemen born', but perhaps there is a satirical glance here at James I's fondness for issuing knighthoods to his loyal supporters, thus elevating them to a higher place in the social hierarchy.

It is also worth remembering that Shakespeare's father's 20-year ambition to achieve gentlemanly status had finally been achieved in 1596 when he was able to acquire a coat of arms, probably as a result of his son's rapidly growing reputation and increasing financial success. Perhaps, even by 1611, Shakespeare still felt a lingering sense of social stigma attached to his provincial background; after all, in 1592 in an envious attack the playwright Robert Greene had described him as an 'upstart crow', which perhaps related as much to his social status as to his lack of a university education. It was Greene whose novel, *Pandosto*, Shakespeare used as the basis of *The Winter's Tale*.

Religion and mythology

England had been a Protestant country since Henry VIII's break with the Roman Catholic Church in the 1530s, despite a brief return to Catholicism under Mary I. The Anglican Church was established under Elizabeth I in 1559, with an episcopal structure — in other words, the bishops were responsible to the crown via parliament. People's real beliefs were left to their individual conscience, but outward conformity was demanded to church attendance and public worship. Up to about 1570, Catholics still outnumbered Protestants and they resented the imputation that they were not loyal to Elizabeth. However, by the later 1570s there was a conviction

that the country had been infiltrated by foreign Catholic priests and members of the Jesuit sect, under the influence of the Pope, who were stirring up disaffection against the queen. In response, anti-Catholic legislation was increased: the fines for recusancy, or refusal to embrace Protestant doctrine, were raised, religious freedom was curtailed and leading Catholics were executed.

James I veered towards Calvinism, a stricter version of Protestantism that espoused particular doctrines such as predestination. The Puritans in particular attempted to adhere closely to Calvinist practice, but neither Elizabeth nor James bowed to their pressure to undertake reforms. Puritanism was frequently ridiculed by Anglicans, but the Puritans saw many elements of superstitious, unscriptural or Catholic practice in Anglican worship. By the 1590s, the Puritans were demanding stricter Sabbath observance and stronger measures against immorality, including the closure of theatres and other places of entertainment. As opposition to the crown grew during the reigns of James I and his son, Charles I, the Puritans became instrumental in the eventual destruction of the monarchy and establishment of a commonwealth after the Civil War. It was these events that marked the closing of the theatres in 1642.

Shakespeare avoids treating doctrinal religious differences in his plays, and indeed it would have been dangerous to do so, particularly if, as many scholars believe, he and his family were secret adherents of the Catholic faith. Moreover, an act was passed in 1606 'for the preventing and avoiding of the great abuse of the Holy Name of God in stage plays', with a £10 fine incurred for every such offence. Companies were given eight days to expurgate their existing plays, though oblique references were acceptable, as in Polixenes's allusion to Judas's betrayal of Christ (I.2.418–19), which does not name either character. Mocking the Puritans did not count as an offence, of course, and playwrights often did so; the Clown, for example, notes that among the shearers who are to sing at the feast, there is 'one puritan [...], and he sings psalms to hornpipes' (IV.3.39–40) — a horrible combination, one is meant to imagine.

Many critics have found an underlying sense of Christian theology in *The Winter's Tale*, despite its ostensibly pagan setting, notably in its powerful structure which follows the central Christian patterning of sin, penance and redemption, with the final stage even marked by a kind of resurrection. The discussion of childhood innocence in Act I scene 2 (lines 67–75) is seen in the context of the doctrine of original sin — 'the imposition [...] | Hereditary ours'; and the play's imagery constantly evokes the idea of 'grace' — a quality which is bestowed by God and leads to salvation. Few, however, would go so far as to interpret the whole play as a Christian allegory, in line with S. L. Bethell's belief that it shows that 'Shakespeare's mature interpretation of life is that of the Christian faith'. There is no doubting, though, that there is a sense of genuine spirituality about the play, from the account given by Cleomenes and Dion of Apollo's oracle in Act III scene 1, steeped in the language of religious ritual, to the mood of 'saint-like sorrow' (V.1.2) that invests Leontes's court in Act V, leading to the transcendental wonder of Hermione's restoration to life. All this is given a convenient distancing from actual engagement with controversial ideas of Christian doctrine by its placing in the context of the classical Roman gods and the allegorical figure of Time. The play's religious sensibilities could not be allowed to come too close to home.

In fact, Christian theology is no more important in the thematic scheme of the play than myth and folklore. In its exploitation of fertility myths, stressing seasonal renewal, the play owes a particular debt to the story of Proserpina, explicitly referred to by Perdita at IV.4.116. Shakespeare could take for granted in his audience a far greater knowledge of Greek and Roman mythology than most people possess now, and the story was a familiar one, best known from Ovid's *Metamorphoses*, which he frequently used as source material. Proserpina (Greek Persephone) was the daughter of Jupiter (Zeus) and Ceres (Demeter). While picking flowers on the isle of Sicily, she was abducted by Dis (or Pluto or Hades), the god of the underworld. As he carried her off, she let her flowers fall, as described by Perdita. Subsequently, she was allowed to return to the earth for six months of each year; in grief, her mother, the goddess of harvests and fertility, decreed that crops should grow only during the period of her daughter's annual return. The relationship of Proserpina's story to the plot of *The Winter's Tale* works suggestively rather than through parallel story lines. The Sicilian link is convenient, the mother's loss of her daughter provides a powerful motive force, and Perdita's life in Bohemia associates her with flowers, fertility and harvest. When Leontes welcomes her and Florizel to Sicilia 'As is the spring to th'earth' (V.1.151), he is explicitly referring to the seasonal regeneration celebrated in the myth.

For Jacobean audiences, the play's mythological and Christian resonances would have worked side by side to create a profoundly spiritual impact without venturing into the dangerous waters of actual church doctrine.

Rural life

Like many of the pastoral settings in Shakespeare's plays — the Forest of Arden in *As You Like It* and the wood near Athens in *A Midsummer Night's Dream* — Bohemia in *The Winter's Tale* is essentially the playwright's native Warwickshire. As a literary genre, pastoral dealt with artificial, unrealistic and idealised country folk, but the rural characters here are decidedly more real. The Shepherd's very first speech reveals him to be in search of two of his best sheep, which he cannot afford to lose, and invests him with a level of wry social awareness that ranges from the irresponsibility of the young to the consequences of illicit sexual liaisons. Sixteen years later, his mysteriously acquired wealth has raised his status; in real life, it was not 'fairy gold' (III.3.108) that had this impact, but the enclosure of common land, which had increased the wealth of some while plunging others into poverty.

Controversially, Shakespeare made money out of the enclosure of land around Stratford-upon-Avon in the later years of his life, and his knowledge of rural affairs is evident in the details he gives of the Shepherd's 'unspeakable estate' (IV.2.32), such as the size of his flock. According to the Clown, this now numbers 'fifteen hundred' (IV.3.31), creating some arithmetical difficulties in his attempt to calculate the prospective income from the shearing. As the Clown speaks, too, of the provisions Perdita has asked him to buy for the feast, the audience would be aware that many of these were luxury items, some of them imported from exotic locations; clearly this was not to be a run-of-the-mill sheep-shearing festival. In all other respects, however, the occasion would have been a recognisable event to rural audiences, but presumably less familiar to the urban patrons of the Globe and the courtly spectators at the Blackfriars.

In contrast to the closely-knit community that has traditionally enjoyed the hospitality of the Shepherd and his family, judging by his account of his late wife's exertions as 'hostess' (IV.4.64) on similar occasions, stands the outsider, Autolycus. In creating him, Shakespeare again combines literary precedent with social reality. There is another debt to Robert Greene, not this time to his prose romance *Pandosto*, which contains no equivalent of Autolycus, but to his *Cony-Catching* pamphlets of 1591–92. In these, Greene claims to expose, from first-hand knowledge, the scams of confidence tricksters and petty criminals. As in Shakespeare's portrayal of Autolycus, there is a certain admiration for their skills, but the social reality was much harsher.

Large numbers of individuals were driven out of the ranks of socialised communities for a variety of reasons, such as population growth, price inflation, enclosure and crop failures, which resulted in a deterioration in the living standards of the poorer working classes. Such people took to the road as vagrants or 'sturdy beggars', their status identified as that of 'masterless men'. Their existence was a cause of considerable social anxiety and, much like today's so-called underclass, they were stereotyped and stigmatised as having rejected the civilised values of respectable society to indulge in lives of easy criminality and sexual promiscuity. With its values based on the household unit and extended family, society viewed beggars and homeless people as a threat to national security, and there were harsh vagrancy laws under which offenders could be literally whipped back to their native parish or sent to houses of correction which involved a regime of hard labour.

Looked at in this way, the jolly, life-enhancing roguery of Autolycus seems to be an unrealistic idealisation of the vagrant life, particularly as, by his own account, his origins lie not in the agricultural labouring classes but as a servant in the royal household. Even so, Shakespeare does not shy away from the reality of life for such social outcasts, and Autolycus admits that 'Gallows and knock are too powerful on the highway. Beating and hanging are terrors to me' (IV.3.27–28). It is entirely characteristic of Shakespeare that he turns the popular conception of vagrants on its head, celebrating the wit and skill with which Autolycus survives by what is essentially criminal dishonesty and deception. Like his real-life counterparts, Autolycus is driven to live like this out of necessity. Perhaps Simon Forman was missing the point, in various ways, when he drew from the 1611 performance of the play, which he saw at the Globe, the principal moral, 'Beware of trusting feigned beggars or fawning fellows'.

Women in society

Despite the example of Queen Elizabeth I, Jacobean society remained firmly patriarchal and, in many respects, misogynistic. Women's choices were almost entirely circumscribed by men, the power exerted by their fathers being taken over on marriage by their husbands. Independent women, like masterless men, were a threat to the social fabric, and those who did not display traditional feminine virtues — modesty, chastity, obedience, mildness — ran the risk of public humiliation or worse. Women were regarded as weak, not merely physically but in their lack of self-control. This belief fed the kind of sexual anxiety that male characters in plays of the time frequently display: it is astonishing how many husbands in Jacobean drama are convinced their wives have been unfaithful to them, as if such sexual promiscuity were inherent in the very fact of being female. Part of the anxiety was a matter of personal dignity: a wronged husband was regarded as a cuckold — a grotesque, horned beast who became an object of mockery and contempt. This is the significance of all those obscure references to horns that abound in Elizabethan and Jacobean drama, often baffling modern audiences. Thus, as Leontes's jealousy takes hold, he talks of 'the infection of my brains | And hard'ning of my brows' (I.2.145–46); comforts himself in the fact that he is not alone, since 'There have been | […] cuckolds ere now' (I.2.190–91); and defines Camillo's obtuseness by suggesting that his 'eye-glass | Is thicker than a cuckold's horn' (I.2.268–69).

Since wives were regarded as their husbands' property, adultery also became a kind of theft. Leontes's 'gates' have been opened against his will; his 'pond' has been fished by his neighbour; and his 'enemy' has penetrated his fortifications 'with bag and baggage' (I.2.194–206). For Leontes, the only comfort is the deeply misogynistic assertion that, 'Should all despair | That have revolted wives, the tenth of mankind | Would hang themselves' (I.2.198–200). There is an echo of this demonisation of women in another of the play's husband and wife relationships, when Antigonus, derided by Leontes for being unable to control his wife's tongue, responds:

> Hang all the husbands
> That cannot do that feat, you'll leave yourself
> Hardly one subject.   (II.3.109–11)

Paulina is here characterised as that other female stereotype, the shrew or the scold, and she comes in for a range of misogynistic abuse from Leontes for the unnaturalness of her conduct, which is unbecoming to a woman and demeaning to her husband. Her behaviour denies her femininity, and in the space of two lines Leontes attaches further anti-feminist stereotypes to her, as a 'mankind witch' and a 'most intelligencing bawd' (II.3.67–68). As a 'mankind', or masculine, woman, she feminises her husband, making him 'woman-tired' and 'unroosted' (II.3.74), a man who 'dreads his wife' (II.3.79) and is even physically abused by her (II.3.90–91). Essentially, her unacceptable behaviour all comes down to her forth-rightness of speech: she is 'lewd-tongued' (II.3.171).

The play itself, of course, does not support or promote such misogynistic stereotyping. Hermione is not an adulteress, Paulina is neither witch nor bawd, and if she is a virago she is so in the defence of truth and justice, and is ultimately the play's agent of moral regeneration. Shakespeare may display in dramatic form the attitudes taken to women in Jacobean society, but he invites his audiences to question and challenge the assumptions of patriarchal authority.

Male friendship

While women were considered fickle and inconstant, arousing undesirable feelings in men and failing to control their own weak passions, male friends, who often referred to each other as brothers, were regarded as beacons of stability and relia-bility. Male friendship, or amity, was idealised almost to the extent of being a cult, and the terms 'love' and 'lover' were used without embarrassment or innuendo to express the feelings engendered in male bonding. Shakespeare explored such rela-tionships persistently throughout his career, from *The Two Gentlemen of Verona*, possibly his earliest play, to *The Two Noble Kinsmen*, one of his last. Friendship is central to his sonnets, and is also illustrated in plays as diverse as *Romeo and Juliet*, *Julius Caesar*, *Much Ado about Nothing* and *Hamlet*. Sometimes one of the friends is an apparently older man who acts as mentor to his younger companion, and modern critics have found undertones of homoerotic attraction in a number of these relationships, notably in *The Merchant of Venice*, *Twelfth Night* and *Troilus and Cressida*, as well as in the sonnets. Though homosexuality was illegal, remaining so until 1967, and in Jacobean times was theoretically punishable by death, in reality the Jacobean court was rife with speculation about same-sex liaisons, and James I himself enjoyed more than close relationships with many of his young courtiers.

Shakespeare makes a point of stressing the friendship of Leontes and Polixenes at the start of *The Winter's Tale*, dating it from their childhoods and even suggesting that it was the influence of the women they were to marry that destroyed their state of innocence. 'We knew not | The doctrine of ill-doing', says Polixenes (I.2.69–70) — at least until their relationships with their future wives began. Hermione picks up his implications and, in a fascinating exchange (I.2.75–86), jokingly suggests that she and Polixenes's queen might be regarded as 'devils' responsible for the 'temp-tations' put in the men's way and causing them, in a sequence of revealing verbs, to trip, sin, slip and 'continue fault' — even though the 'offences' she is talking about are nothing more than sexual relations within marriage. The sin, one feels, lay in the potential breaking up of a male friendship.

Yet Leontes and Polixenes's friendship has survived marriage, time and physical distance, as Camillo makes clear in the first scene. In such a context of idealised male bonding, betrayal of one's friend is unthinkable, on the level of Judas's betrayal of Christ, as Polixenes points out (I.2.417–19). Polixenes's interpretation of how Leontes must feel climaxes not in the impact of his wife's supposed unfaithfulness, but in his having been 'dishonoured by a man which ever | Professed to him' (I.2.455–56). When their friendship is rekindled at the end of the play, it seems odd that Polixenes takes the blame for their estrangement on himself as 'him that was the cause of this' (V.3.54). Only in the Renaissance cult of amity does this make sense, but it pales into insignificance beside a parallel moment at the climax of *The Two Gentlemen of Verona*. Proteus has fallen in love with Valentine's girlfriend Silvia, has deviously contrived Valentine's banishment and, when Silvia spurns his advances, has attempted to rape her. When he apologises, Valentine not only forgives him, but offers him Silvia as well. Nothing could demonstrate more clearly how male friendship is simply another variant on patriarchal control.

Elizabethan and Jacobean theatre

London's first purpose-built theatre was erected in 1576 in Shoreditch by James Burbage. Simply called The Theatre, it marked the start of probably the richest period of dramatic creativity seen in Britain until well into the twentieth century. Previous theatrical companies had had no permanent performance spaces, touring their shows to halls, inn-yards and public spaces; they were regarded as vagrants or beggars if they did not have lordly patronage. There was also a tradition of non-professional performances in the universities, and at the Inns of Court, where lawyers were trained.

By the time Shakespeare was at the height of his success, London had a variety of theatrical companies playing across a range of theatres, both outdoor and indoor. The most prestigious of these companies had operated as the Lord Chamberlain's Men during the last years of Queen Elizabeth's reign; they opened their Globe Theatre in 1599 and acquired royal patronage on the accession of James I, becoming the King's Men in 1603. Their chief rivals were Prince Henry's Men, formerly the Admiral's Men, based at the nearby Rose. Great performers had established popular reputations, from the tragic actors Edward Alleyn and Richard Burbage to the comedians Richard Tarlton and Will Kemp. Two generations of dramatists had provided increasingly sophisticated plays in a variety of genres. Christopher Marlowe and Thomas Kyd, as well as Shakespeare, had established their reputations in the 1580s, and Ben Jonson, Thomas Middleton, Thomas Dekker,

George Chapman, John Marston and Thomas Heywood were among those who gained popularity in the early years of King James's reign. Plays such as Marlowe's *The Jew of Malta* and Kyd's *The Spanish Tragedy* were perennial favourites, and Shakespeare's plays were regularly among those chosen by royal command for performances at court.

If you have visited the reconstructed Globe Theatre in London, on the south bank of the Thames at Southwark, a few hundred yards from its original site, you may have gained the impression that we know a great deal about the playhouses of Elizabethan and Jacobean London, and how plays were staged there. In fact, we know surprisingly little. Our classic image of an Elizabethan theatre, so vividly portrayed in films such as Laurence Olivier's *Henry V* (1944) or John Madden's *Shakespeare in Love* (1998), is based on calculated guesswork — a set of assumptions and conjectures derived from comparatively limited documentary evidence and a few archaeological remains. Only one contemporary drawing of an Elizabethan theatre, the Swan, survives (reproduced above) — and that is of somewhat doubtful accuracy.

Mary Evans Picture Library

We do have some architectural specifications for the building of new theatres such as the second Globe, which replaced the original after it was destroyed by fire in 1613. The notebooks of the successful theatrical manager Philip Henslowe provide fascinating information on a range of practical and economic theatrical issues, from inventories of stage properties to payments for the services of writers. There are also a few accounts of theatre performances, some by visiting foreign diplomats. Much of what we know about theatrical practice, however, has to be inferred from the actual texts of the plays that were performed — and hundreds of these have not survived.

A number of points that are important to understand in order to grasp certain features of the plays of the Elizabethan and Jacobean period are outlined below:

- The public playhouses were open-air amphitheatres holding 2,000–3,000 spectators. They may have been modelled on the inn-yards where plays had often been performed in the past.

- The stage was a raised wooden platform thrust into the yard or pit. It was covered by a canopy, probably supported by two pillars.
- Stage features included a curtained-off alcove or recess at the back, flanked by two doors for entrances and exits, with a balcony above.
- Entrances (and exits) were also possible through a trap-door, and the more sophisticated theatres could fly in actors from above.
- Performances took place in the afternoon, and were lit by daylight.
- Props and furniture were used, but sets were minimal. Setting and atmosphere had to be created where necessary in the words of the script.
- Costumes were splendid and elaborate, but little effort was made to match them to the period of the play; instead, they would reflect character and status.
- Music was an important part of the performance, and there was also a range of sound and other special effects, from thunder to fireworks.
- Women were not allowed to act, so female parts were taken by boys. Some roles, such as the witches in *Macbeth* or the Nurse in *Romeo and Juliet*, were probably played by men.
- Audiences came from the whole social range. Those who could afford to pay more sat in the galleries; others stood in the yard.
- Many people in the audience would have had a restricted view of the stage. People generally spoke of going to *hear* a play rather than going to *see* one. The emphasis was therefore on the spoken text.
- Plays were often performed at court by royal command, and they could be adapted easily to different venues.
- There were a number of private indoor theatres, lit by candles, which catered for a more educated, courtly audience. These were mostly occupied by companies of boy actors.
- The King's Men did not perform regularly in an indoor theatre until 1609, when they opened the Blackfriars as their winter home.
- The needs of the Blackfriars, such as regular intervals for trimming the candles, had an effect on the dramatic structuring of play scripts.

Shakespeare's life, works and theatrical career

What little we know about Shakespeare's life has been filled out with centuries of conjecture, which means that it is sometimes difficult to separate fact from fiction. His parents were prosperous and respected Warwickshire tradespeople, living in Stratford-upon-Avon. William was born in 1564, possibly on 23 April, and in the next 15 years his parents had three more sons and two daughters. He presumably attended local schools, and at the grammar school would have received a solid

grounding in Latin, classical literature and rhetoric. At the age of 18 he married Anne Hathaway, from the nearby village of Shottery; she was six years older than him, and already expecting their first child, Susanna, who was born in May 1583. Their twins, Hamnet and Judith, followed in February 1585.

From this point, there are no further records of Shakespeare's life until 1592, by which time he was established as a playwright in London. This period, often referred to as 'the lost years', has fuelled many imaginative speculations: perhaps he was a schoolmaster in the north of England; or maybe he joined the theatrical company the Queen's Men, who played in Stratford in 1587, after one of their leading actors was killed in a duel. All we know is that by 1592 he had written a number of plays, including *The Two Gentlemen of Verona*, *The Taming of the Shrew*, *The Comedy of Errors*, the three parts of *Henry VI*, *Richard III* and *Titus Andronicus*, sometimes collaborating with other writers, and that he had aroused the envy of another playwright, Robert Greene, who referred to him as 'an upstart crow [who] is in his own conceit the only Shake-scene in a country'. We do not know which companies Shakespeare worked for at this time, nor at which theatres, but it is likely that some of his plays were presented at The Theatre in Shoreditch, run by the Burbage family.

Shortly after this, the London theatres were closed by a particularly virulent outbreak of plague, and Shakespeare turned his hand to poetry, publishing *Venus and Adonis* and *The Rape of Lucrece*, both dedicated to the young nobleman Henry Wriothesley, Earl of Southampton. By 1594, though, he had become a shareholder in a theatre company, which had now won the patronage of the Lord Chamberlain. The lease on the Shoreditch Theatre had run out, and the Chamberlain's Men performed mostly at the Curtain. Shakespeare himself was now living in St Helen's parish, in the City of London.

However, Shakespeare had not severed his links with his family and friends in Stratford. His son Hamnet died in 1596 at the age of 11, and in the same year his father John's long-held ambition to be granted the honour of a coat of arms, raising him to the status of gentleman, was finally successful, perhaps reflecting William's public success; both these events seem to be recalled in *The Winter's Tale*. He also invested in a new Stratford home, buying one of the town's biggest houses, New Place, in 1597. In 1598, his plays, which by now included *Romeo and Juliet*, *Love's Labour's Lost*, *A Midsummer Night's Dream*, *Richard II*, *The Merchant of Venice*, the two parts of *Henry IV*, *The Merry Wives of Windsor* and *King John*, were praised in print by Francis Meres as 'the most excellent' in English, for both comedy and tragedy.

In 1599, the Lord Chamberlain's Men dismantled the Shoreditch Theatre and used its timbers to build the Globe Theatre on Bankside, in Southwark, where Shakespeare himself probably now lived. *Henry V* and *Julius Caesar* were almost certainly written for the new Globe; other plays produced in this period were *Much Ado about Nothing*, *As You Like It*, *Twelfth Night* and *Hamlet*. Back in Stratford, Shakespeare's father died in 1601, and the playwright made the first of a series of investments in local land and property. His fame at this time is demonstrated by the circulation of gossipy stories about him, including his sexual exploits.

Queen Elizabeth died in 1603 and was succeeded by the theatre-loving James I, who took over the patronage of Shakespeare's company, which became the King's Men. Command performances at court thus became an even more regular feature of their programme. The next six years represented the height of the King's Men's success and Shakespeare's dramatic career. He focused his attention on tragedies, including *Othello*, *King Lear*, *Macbeth*, *Antony and Cleopatra* and *Coriolanus*, and on dark comedies, such as *Troilus and Cressida*, *Measure for Measure* and *All's Well that Ends Well*. He also collaborated with Thomas Middleton on *Timon of Athens*. We know that in 1604 Shakespeare was lodging with a Huguenot family, the Mountjoys, in north London, and that in 1607 his daughter Susanna married the respected Stratford physician, John Hall. His brother Edmund, a successful actor, died in this year, and was buried in what is now Southwark Cathedral.

At the height of his success, Shakespeare published his collection of sonnets, which had been circulating privately for some years, and a key event in his theatrical career was his company's adoption in 1609 of the indoor Blackfriars Theatre as its winter home. The romantic tragicomedies, *Pericles*, *Cymbeline*, *The Winter's Tale* and *The Tempest* were written partly to cater for the different aesthetic of the indoor theatre, and partly to respond to changes in theatrical taste. Shakespeare also collaborated with his younger colleague John Fletcher, who was to take over from him as the King's Men's chief dramatist, on *The Two Noble Kinsmen* and *Cardenio*; the text of the latter is now lost.

In 1612, Shakespeare's brother Gilbert died, and he was called on to testify in a court case relating to his former landlords, the Mountjoys. In 1613 he was investing in property in the Blackfriars area, but disaster came on 29 June when the Globe burned down during a performance of *All Is True* (or *Henry VIII*), a Shakespeare/Fletcher collaboration. Even though the theatre was rebuilt within a year, this effectively marked the end of Shakespeare's theatrical career, and it is usually assumed that he subsequently retired to Stratford. Here, he was involved in disputes about unpopular land enclosures, and in the marriage of his daughter Judith to the unreliable Thomas Quiney. Shakespeare died on 23 April 1616, aged 52, and was buried two days later in a prime position in Stratford's Holy Trinity Church. Among the beneficiaries of Shakespeare's will were his theatrical colleagues, John Heminges and Henry Condell, who later edited the first collected edition of his works, subsequently known as the First Folio, which was published in 1623 — the year in which his widow, Anne, died. Copies of the Folio sold for £1 each.

Genre and theatrical context

When Shakespeare began work around 1608 on what we now think of as his last plays, he was striking out in a new direction. Since the turn of the century he had focused on a series of powerful but diverse tragedies; he had interspersed these with two dark, ironic comedies, *Measure for Measure* and *All's Well that Ends Well*, exploring complex moral issues with only partial or ambiguous resolutions, and with the bitterly satirical drama of love and war, *Troilus and Cressida*. In the plays that followed, though, the potential for tragedy is diverted into a series of positive outcomes, as Shakespeare embraces the increasingly popular genre of tragicomedy. These plays, *Pericles, Cymbeline, The Winter's Tale* and *The Tempest*, have a great deal in common with each other, including some striking verbal echoes.

Tragicomedy has long been regarded as an inferior or bastard genre, lacking both the joyous exuberance of comedy and the philosophical seriousness of tragedy. As a result, Shakespeare's move into this genre has often been seen as a decline, explained by either a surfeit of tragic despair or a slackening of his intellectual powers.

Such a view, however, ignores something crucial about Shakespeare: he was a practical and experienced theatrical businessman with shares in his company, the King's Men, on whose success his financial security depended. It is unlikely that he thought of these as his 'last plays'; much more probable is that he was responding to the economic conditions and changes in fashion evident in the contemporary theatrical world. Such influences on these plays probably included the following factors:

- In 1609 the King's Men took possession of the indoor Blackfriars Theatre, attracting a more educated and courtly 'private' audience.
- Performances at the Blackfriars were lit by candles. As these had to be trimmed at regular intervals, plays were increasingly constructed in five acts, in contrast to the continuous performances that were normal in the outdoor playhouses, which allowed for less artificially structured plays.
- The courtly audience would be familiar with the increasingly fashionable masques presented before royalty. These were elaborately-staged entertainments combining poetry, music, song, dance and scenic spectacle, and were written by theatre practitioners such as Ben Jonson. The Blackfriars therefore probably used more scenic effects than the Globe, and the plays contained specifically masque-like elements, such as the descent of Jupiter in *Cymbeline*, sitting on an eagle and throwing a thunderbolt. The dance of the satyrs in *The Winter's Tale* may have been 'borrowed' from Jonson's *Masque of Oberon* earlier in 1611.

The influence of the Blackfriars should not be exaggerated, however, since it served largely as the King's Men's winter home, with plays in its repertoire being performed at the Globe too in the summer months. Simon Forman saw *The Winter's Tale* at the Globe in May 1611, and that theatre's stage machinery was certainly sophisticated enough to cope with the special effects required in these plays. The less courtly members of the Globe audience may well have derived a particular *frisson* from being allowed to share in something of the nature of the court masques from which they were excluded.

The genre of tragicomedy had been much debated in literary and dramatic circles, particularly since the appearance of an English translation of Giambattista Guarini's *The Faithful Shepherd* in 1602, and there was a renewed interest in it as a dramatic mode by the end of the decade. The King's Men, in particular, led the fashion in this respect, not only with Shakespeare's plays but with other popular works such as Beaumont and Fletcher's *Philaster* (1609) and *A King and No King* (1611); other companies soon joined the bandwagon.

Associated with tragicomedy were the literary modes of romance, dealing with unrealistic episodes often involving lovers; and pastoral, set in an idealised country landscape inhabited by shepherds and their flocks. Both modes can be seen at work in *The Winter's Tale*, though Shakespeare had used them much earlier in *As You Like It* (1600), a play that has a great deal in common with these later works. The plot of *The Winter's Tale* also contains strong parallels with another earlier comedy, *Much Ado about Nothing* (1598–99).

Shakespeare's use of Time as the chorus to *The Winter's Tale* points up another issue about genre. It is implicit in his speech that healing and regeneration are not the end — merely the arbitrary conclusion imposed for the purposes of the genres known as 'comedy' or 'tragicomedy'. Time makes it clear that he controls 'both joy and terror | Of good and bad', and that he 'makes' as well as 'unfolds' error (IV.1.1–2). If *Othello* had ended with the hero's successful marriage to Desdemona, or *King Lear* with the reunion of Lear and Cordelia, they would be comedies. Equally, if *The Winter's Tale* concluded with Act III scene 2 it would be a tragedy. Shakespeare ends most of his comedies with a sense that the comedic closure is only provisional, undercutting the final harmony with unsettling elements. How does Isabella respond to the Duke's proposal at the end of *Measure for Measure*? Why are characters like Malvolio in *Twelfth Night*, Antonio in *The Merchant of Venice* or Jaques in *As You Like It* excluded from full participation in the positive ending? What kind of a marriage is in store for Benedick and Beatrice in *Much Ado about Nothing* or Helena and Bertram in *All's Well that Ends Well*? 'All yet seems well' says the King at the end of that play; perhaps the same linguistic qualification — 'seems' rather than 'is' — needs to be applied to all of Shakespeare's so-called 'happy endings', including *The Winter's Tale*. The commentary on Act V scene 3 examines some of the ambiguous undercurrents that potentially darken the resolution of this play.

Shakespeare's last plays

Presumably, when Shakespeare began writing *Pericles* in about 1607–08, he did not consciously consider that he was embarking upon his final sequence of plays. In retrospect, however, critics have seen it as the first of a group of related works with which he closed his career as a dramatist. The plays in this group consist essentially of the four 'romances', *Pericles, Cymbeline, The Winter's Tale* and *The Tempest*. The history play *All Is True* (*Henry VIII*) is frequently added to this group, despite being a collaboration with John Fletcher. *The Two Noble Kinsmen*, also a Fletcher–Shakespeare collaboration, is less often considered in this context.

Dating these plays is difficult. On their supposed artistic merits, the traditional view was that *Pericles* was written first, almost as an experiment in a new genre; then followed *Cymbeline*, in which the experiment achieved greater success; next came *The Winter's Tale*, which was better still; and finally *The Tempest*, Shakespeare's final non-collaborative play, the artistic climax of this group, and his effective farewell to the theatre. Modern scholarship has questioned this chronology, however, putting *The Winter's Tale* before *Cymbeline*, and *Pericles* even before *Coriolanus*, his last great tragedy. There are also those who consider *Cymbeline* and *The Winter's Tale* to be more dramatically effective than *The Tempest*. *Pericles* is a particular problem inasmuch as it was not included in the First Folio of 1623, and exists only in an unreliable, somewhat garbled individual text, which probably doesn't represent the play as originally written and performed. It is also considered to be a collaboration, perhaps with George Wilkins, who later wrote a novel based on the story.

Whatever the uncertainties, there can be no doubt of the many similarities between these plays, some of which are outlined below. However, these parallels have perhaps been given too much weight in the past, obscuring the fact that the differences between the plays are just as striking as their similarities; and that there are also frequent parallels with plays written much earlier in Shakespeare's career.

The principal parallels between these plays lie in their plots, characters, themes and imagery. Children are separated from their royal parents, often in ignorance of their own true identities, but finally reunited. Evil acts committed in corrupt courtly societies are mitigated by a transfer of the characters to idealised rural landscapes or remote islands. The qualities of particular flowers are celebrated as they are 'strewn' on the dead and the living. Characters repent their sins and are rewarded by recon-ciliation with those they wronged, including at least three wives and one husband who had been thought dead. Characters are battered by storm and tempest, but the elements that threatened eventually prove merciful. Dreams, visions and prophecies relate the stories to a legendary world ruled by the gods: Diana and Jupiter make dramatic personal appearances, Apollo's voice is heard through his Oracle, and Iris, Ceres and Juno are conjured up in a magical wedding celebration. Loyal old coun-sellors stand firm against tyranny and offer moral guidance and practical advice. The mistakes of the old are rectified by the love and energy of their children. Tragedy is shown to be only a partial response to a life in which the natural cycle brings rebirth, regeneration or, as Leontes calls it, 'recreation' (III.2.237). Winter must always be succeeded by spring. The happy endings, though, remain provisional: not all those who die along the way can be reborn, and not all the evil characters can be brought to embrace repentance and forgiveness.

Sources of the play

The term sources is perhaps a misleading one. It suggests that a writer creates a literary or dramatic work while surrounded by a variety of other texts, reshaping their plots, characters, ideas and language into something new and distinctive. Sometimes this is undoubtedly true, but sources often work in a less organised, more amorphous way, taking in memories and recollections, personal experience, contemporary cultural preoccupations and current events, in addition to the more specific influence of other plays, stories, poems and historical accounts.

In the narrow sense of the term, Shakespeare's principal source for *The Winter's Tale* is a prose romance by Robert Greene, probably first published in 1588, entitled *Pandosto: The Triumph of Time*. The subtitle suggests the author's moral or philosophical purpose, which is made more explicit further on in the title page: 'Although by the means of sinister fortune Truth may be concealed, yet by Time, in spite of fortune, it is most manifestly revealed'. Later editions changed the title to *The History of Dorastus and Fawnia*, altering the focus from the jealous Pandosto (the equivalent of Leontes) to the young lovers, recreated by Shakespeare as Florizel and Perdita.

Why do scholars attach importance to an examination of Shakespeare's sources? This is a good question, since a text should surely stand by itself, able to be appreciated without reference to the influences that helped to shape it. Often, though, such a comparison can be revealing. Omissions, additions and changes of emphasis can help us to see something of Shakespeare's intentions and to appreciate the effects he created in fashioning a new work.

In *The Winter's Tale*, Shakespeare follows the essential story-line of *Pandosto* closely, and there are frequent echoes of Greene's language and phrasing. The overall effect of Shakespeare's play is quite different, however, as one would expect from a story that needs to be told in dramatic and theatrical terms through character and dialogue. Some of the key differences are outlined below.

- Shakespeare gives much greater emphasis and development to the two vitally contrasting emotional landscapes of his story: the jealousy of Leontes and the sheep-shearing celebrations, the latter developed from the merest hint in Greene. He also reverses the geographical settings, switching round Bohemia and Sicilia.
- Hermione's 'resurrection', the moving climax of Shakespeare's play, is his own invention. Her equivalent in Pandosto, Bellaria, genuinely dies after her trial;

consequently, at the end of the story, after having been reunited with his daughter, there is no prospect of a new life for the repentant Pandosto, who commits suicide.

- Paulina, as stage-manager of Hermione's survival, therefore has no equivalent in Greene's story. She is one of the most memorable characters in the play and is entirely Shakespeare's.
- Other major characters added by Shakespeare are Antigonus and the Clown. Autolycus, whose amoral vitality is so crucial to the impact of the Bohemian scenes of the play, is also largely Shakespeare's invention. His roguery probably owes something to the rascals and vagabonds portrayed by Greene in his *Cony-Catching* pamphlets.
- Shakespeare's resolution is only partly achieved by Time, and much more by the human qualities — love, loyalty and self-sacrifice — of characters such as Paulina, Camillo, Perdita and Florizel. Though Shakespeare adds a personification of Time as the chorus, he is an old-fashioned, partly comic figure, reminding the audience of the old morality plays.

Perhaps Shakespeare is also partly mocking Robert Greene. Six years older than Shakespeare, the Cambridge-educated writer had been a successful playwright in the early 1590s, when Shakespeare was starting out on his writing career. Best known for *Friar Bacon and Friar Bungay* (1589) and *James IV* (1590), he also collaborated with other dramatists and may have worked with Shakespeare. At any rate, he appears to have become envious of the younger, less-educated writer's success, penning a famous put-down in his *Groatsworth of Wit*, written as he lay dying in squalor and penury in 1592. In it, he warns his fellow university-trained writers to beware of 'an upstart crow, beautified with our feathers, that […] supposes he is as well able to bombast out a blank verse as the best of you; and […] is in his own conceit the only Shake-scene in a country'.

It seems unlikely that Shakespeare would wait 20 years and then respond so obliquely to Greene's attack by transforming his rather dull romance into an effective stage-play. However, in the play's title and its references to old tales, perhaps Shakespeare is slyly suggesting that Greene's story is as out of date as the old-fashioned plays which he mocks in 'The Murder of Gonzago' in *Hamlet* and the ghost scene in *Cymbeline*. Nevertheless, *Pandosto* was reprinted yet again in 1614 — maybe in the wake of *The Winter's Tale's* success.

The printed text

The Winter's Tale, in common with another 15 of his plays, was not published in Shakespeare's lifetime. It first appeared in print in Heminges and Condell's collected edition of Shakespeare's works, now known as the First Folio, in 1623. However, it is a mistake to think that the Folio printing represents the play 'as Shakespeare intended it'. The text went through many other hands before it ended up in its printed form including:

- The theatre company, which would have created a prompt-book for running performances in the playhouse.
- Possibly other writers, who may have made alterations and adaptations to the play for later performances after Shakespeare's death in 1616.
- A scribe, in this case probably Ralph Crane, who made a fair copy for the printers to use, working either from Shakespeare's original manuscript (which may not always have been easily legible), or from the theatre's prompt-book. Crane had his own peculiar habits, for example in listing all the characters who were to appear in a scene at the beginning of that scene, whether or not they actually entered then or later.
- The printing-house staff, including compositors and proof-readers, who might well have introduced their own changes, either accidentally or deliberately, following their own particular preferences for spelling and punctuation.

Thus, even the First Folio is a collaborative version of the play, and should not be taken as sacrosanct.

However, it is much easier for a modern editor to work on *The Winter's Tale* than on a text such as *Hamlet* or *King Lear*, which had already been printed individually before being published in the First Folio. There are often huge differences between the versions of these plays published at different times, giving modern editors an enormous, if not impossible, task. The three printed versions of *Hamlet* and two of *King Lear* are so different as almost to amount to separate plays.

Even in *The Winter's Tale*, the text you are studying, whichever modern edition you are using, will be different in many respects from the Folio version and from other modern editions. The principal changes made by editors are as follows:

- correcting obvious misprints
- using a modern typeface, thereby eliminating letter-forms in the original such as the long s, u for v and vice versa, and i for j
- altering spelling and punctuation to conform to modern conventions
- identifying apparent errors and difficulties in the Folio text and attempting to provide a reading that makes sense
- rationalising stage directions to give a clearer idea of the action happening on stage
- adding line numbers to each scene — these may be different in different editions, because lines of prose occupy varying amounts of space depending on the format of the edition and the typeface used

Many of these editorial practices, however, are acts of interpretation as much as clarification, and can have a variety of problematic effects:

- Changing the way a sentence is punctuated can alter its meaning, shift its emphasis or remove deliberate ambiguities.

- Modernising spelling can obscure the Jacobean pronunciation, perhaps eliminating subtle effects of assonance or onomatopoeia.
- Fixing stage directions can limit a reader's awareness of alternative ways of staging a scene.

Virtually all modern editions of *The Winter's Tale* make two changes to the Folio text in Act V. At V.3.18, the Folio prints 'Lovely', which is commonly changed to 'Lonely'. And at V.3.96, the Cambridge Schools edition is unusual in beginning the line with the Folio reading, 'On', which most editors change to 'Or'. Small as they seem, these common changes to the Folio text are significant acts of editorial reinterpretation.

Despite these reservations, most modern editions avoid the excesses of editors in the eighteenth and nineteenth centuries, whose interventions, such as stating explicitly where each scene was supposed to take place, presented a misleading and limiting view of how the plays work, both reflecting and influencing the elaborately pictorial Shakespearean productions of those centuries.

You should get into the habit of using your edition critically and questioning its assumptions. If you always think of the text as a blueprint for a theatrical perform-ance, with all the staging alternatives that this implies, you cannot go far wrong.

Scene summaries and commentary

As with all parts of this guide, you should use this section critically. It is not a substitute for your own close reading of the text: there are other angles and inter-pretations which are not considered here. Question everything you read and weigh it against your own understanding of each scene. The commentary in particular is highly selective. It cannot cover every aspect of every scene, and the focus here is usually on character, with regular reflections on themes, language and staging possibilities.

Act I scene 1

Archidamus, in conversation with Camillo, praises the hospitality the Bohemian visitors have received in the Sicilian court, and doubts if his own country could match it if a return visit were paid. They discuss the longstanding friendship of their kings, dating from childhood, and the admirable qualities of the young Sicilian prince, Mamillius, who inspires the people with a sense of wellbeing.

Opening scenes are crucial in imparting important background information to the audience. Shakespeare often begins, as here, with two subsidiary characters discussing the social and political situation. Archidamus remains anonymous in the dialogue and never reappears, whereas Camillo develops into a major supporting character throughout the play. Like the two Roman soldiers whose dialogue opens *Antony and Cleopatra*, and who never appear again, Archidamus is a dramatic device rather than a fully developed character.

Camillo and Archidamus converse in courtly prose. Their discourse is polite, artificial and rhetorical, full of verbal flourishes such as false modesty and hyperbole, as when Archidamus suggests that, if the Sicilians were to visit Bohemia, their hosts would have to drug them to conceal the inadequacy of their hospitality. These two men are not friends; their dialogue suggests emotional distance, perhaps a degree of insincerity. The polite surface of their polished prose forms a striking contrast with the passionate and emotional verse that is to be released in the next scene.

As well as imparting information, Shakespeare uses the opening scene to establish some of the play's key images. In particular, the central opposition of youth and old age is explored through the account of Leontes and Polixenes's childhood friendship, and through the curative power of Mamillius to make 'old hearts fresh'. Retrospectively, however, the discussion is invested with a sad irony in view of Mamillius's subsequent fate. There is irony, too, in Camillo's plea for 'the heavens' to 'continue' the love between Polixenes and Leontes, and Archidamus's forcefully alliterative reply that there is neither 'malice or matter' in the world to alter it. An attentive listener to this exchange, even if unaware of the course the story is to take, might suspect that the very strength of these assertions is a hint that something will, in fact, go drastically wrong between the two kings.

To modern tastes, an expository dialogue between two courtiers does not seem a particularly dramatic start to the play, and directors have often enlivened the opening by placing Camillo and Archidamus against a lively celebratory background of busy court activity. This has the advantage of enabling them to refer to the two kings by gesture and expression, thus introducing them visually to the audience. Bringing Mamillius on stage to prompt Archidamus's first reference to him can also help to animate the dialogue.

Act I scene 2

After nine months in Sicilia, Polixenes is anxious to return home, but Leontes tries to talk him into extending his visit, if only by a few days. At Leontes's request, Hermione, who is in the late stages of pregnancy, joins in his attempts at persuasion, and is soon successful; as Leontes observes from a distance, the conversation between Hermione and Polixenes turns to the boyhood friendship of the two kings. Leontes returns to the conversation and praises Hermione's powers of persuasion; leaving them again, however, he is overcome with jealousy, even seeking reassurance from Mamillius that he is indeed his son. Noting his agitation, Hermione and Polixenes inquire what is troubling him; he claims to have been inspired by Mamillius to reflect on his own childhood, and the talk turns to Polixenes's son, before he and Hermione leave to walk in the garden. After another passionately jealous outburst, Leontes sends Mamillius off to play and engages Camillo in conversation, demanding to know his thoughts on Hermione's success in getting Polixenes to stay longer. Camillo is astonished by Leontes's assertions of Hermione's infidelity and vigorously defends her, but responds equivocally to the king's demand that he poison Polixenes. He eventually promises to do it providing no action is subsequently taken against the queen. Left alone, Camillo determines to disobey the king and abandon the court; he reluctantly tells everything to Polixenes, who has returned wondering why Leontes has just cut him dead. Camillo urges Polixenes to escape while he has the chance, and pledges his services to him.

The pace of this long scene is impressively swift, moving with gripping intensity from domestic harmony to disruption and fragmentation. The speed and suddenness with which Leontes's jealousy takes hold has aroused centuries of critical debate. Comparisons with *Othello* are interesting but ultimately unhelpful since, although Othello's jealousy develops almost as quickly, it is instigated and nurtured by Iago's devious malevolence; Leontes's jealousy, on the contrary, is entirely self-generated. An actor needs to decide whether Leontes is already jealous before the scene begins, or whether his suspicions descend on him as the action unfolds. Evidence for the former is provided by the almost monosyllabic brusqueness of his contributions to the dialogue at the start of the scene, and certainly the unpleasant imagery of his reflections on his wooing of Hermione – 'crabbèd', 'soured', 'death' – forms a suggestive prelude to his first outburst at line 108. Perhaps, though, this outburst is meant to seem entirely spontaneous, like a bolt from the blue. Critics who argue that this is psychologically unconvincing are taking a modern view of both psychology and drama: characters in plays need not behave as people do in real life, and characterisation in Renaissance drama can often seem superficial, inconsistent and discontinuous by modern standards. In performance, there is no doubt that this scene always works powerfully, as we accept the play on its own terms.

The language of Leontes's jealous outbursts is passionate and violent, providing a striking contrast with both the calm, measured fluency of Polixenes and Hermione's lively and attractive wit. In Leontes's speeches, the verse rhythms are often irregular and fractured, the grammatical structures complicated and parenthetical. Even so, the beat of the iambic pentameter still powerfully underlies the verse in regular lines such as 'To mingle friendship far is mingling bloods', often emphasised, as here, by repetition. Alliterative effects combine with assonance to create the onomatopoeic spitting and hissing of his intemperate passion: 'paddling palms and pinching fingers'; 'Inch-thick, knee-deep'; 'whose issue | Will hiss me to my grave'; 'sluiced in's absence'.

With such an intense focus on Leontes, it is easy to overlook the other characters, stereotyping them merely as models of virtue. It is certainly important that we are in no doubt about Hermione's integrity, which is emphatically presented through the Christian terminology of 'grace'. The word itself is on her lips three times in the space of 25 lines, while both Camillo and Polixenes refer to her as 'gracious'. Yet she does not have to be presented as a paragon, and an actor can make her more human by stressing a slightly irritating quality in some of her bantering wit. In her speech, 'What, have I twice said well?', for example, her insistent, affectionate sarcasm might be shown to demonstrate insensitivity to her husband's mood; or, conversely, to reveal her overcompensating for the tenseness she has noticed in his demeanour.

It is easy, too, to take Polixenes and Camillo at face value, when perhaps Shakespeare subtly invites us to question certain aspects of their behaviour. If, for example, Polixenes loves his young son so much, how can he justify having abandoned him, not to mention his country, for nine months? 'My affairs | Do even drag me homeward,' he says, the language suggesting a reluctance to resume his responsibilities. And what are we to make of Camillo and Polixenes's flight from danger at the end of the scene? 'I | Have uttered truth,' says Camillo, 'which if you seek to prove, | I dare not stand by,' while Polixenes admits, 'Fear o'ershades me.' Instead of confronting Leontes, or warning Hermione, they leave her to her fate, reminding us perhaps of the Friar's abandoning of Juliet at the climax of *Romeo and Juliet* with the line, 'I dare no longer stay'. Remembering their moral cowardice here, it becomes easier to accept their dubious behaviour in relation to Florizel in the second part of the play, spying on him in disguise rather than being frank and open.

This scene is dense with powerfully emotive patterns of imagery, of which the most noticeable is perhaps the idea of disease. From the 'tremor cordis' that Leontes experiences at the outbreak of his jealousy, he sees his imagined transformation into a cuckold, his brow sprouting that creature's horns, in terms of an 'infection' of his brains, and comments that thousands of husbands 'have the disease and feel't not'. For him, the origin of the disease lies in Hermione's supposed infidelity: 'Were my wife's liver | Infected as her life, she would not live | The running of one glass'. The image of the hourglass here connects with another important strand of imagery developed in the scene through its frequent references to time, later to be given concrete embodiment in the Act IV chorus. From units of time – 'nine changes of the wat'ry star', 'one sev'night', 'a month', 'a week', 'hours', 'minutes' – to specific moments – 'tomorrow', 'today', 'noon', midnight'; from the clocks and hourglasses that measure time, to the concept of 'perpetuity' and eternity, Time's controlling power in human life is stressed.

Disease, though, remains the more noticeable idea in the scene, and when it is taken up by Camillo and Polixenes in a number of references stressing its infectious quality, its origin is firmly located in Leontes's jealous obsession, his 'diseased opinion', even though Camillo suggests at one point that it has been 'caught' from Polixenes, healthy as he is. Responding to this, Polixenes wishes the symptoms on himself: 'O then my best blood turn | To an infected jelly'. At present there is no remedy, despite Camillo's urging of Leontes to 'be cured | Of this diseased opinion'. There is, however, a potential cure which in the first part of the play is impotent and inoperative, embodied in the power of childhood innocence. Employing the seasonal imagery which is also so important in the overall scheme of the play, Polixenes states that his young son:

> makes a July's day short as December,
> And with his varying childness cures in me
> Thoughts that would thick my blood.

In response, Leontes claims that Mamillius has the same effect on him: 'So stands this squire | Officed with me'; a remark that is filled with a sad and profound irony, since the child is clearly exerting no such curative power on his father's obsessive jealousy.

The reflections on childhood and maturity are often seen in terms of innocence and experience. Growing into adulthood is defined by Polixenes as an increasing awareness of sin, and his discussion with Hermione between lines 67 and 86 is crammed with suggestions of evil and temptation, sin and guilt, referring explicitly to the Biblical doctrine of original sin – 'the imposition [...] | Hereditary ours' – told in the story of Adam and Eve. Other explicit Christian references connect with this, such as Polixenes's allusion to Judas, in claiming that, if he is guilty, his name will be linked 'with his that did betray the Best'. These Christian references, in a play that later embraces the pagan Apollo and his oracle, seem odd, but have led some commentators to interpret the whole play in the light of Christian theology.

In subtle touches, Shakespeare anticipates his later presentation of Bohemia as essentially a pastoral economy through incidental images in the speech of Polixenes, from his reference to 'the shepherd's note' in his opening speech to his comparison of Leontes and himself as children to 'twinned lambs that did frisk i'th'sun | And bleat the one at th'other'. In more ominous hints of later developments, Shakespeare two or three times uses images of imprisonment, anticipating Hermione's imminent incarceration.

This is a rich and complex scene, overlaying its dramatic events with webs and patterns of suggestive imagery, only a few examples of which have been dealt with in this commentary.

Act II scene 1

Unaware of imminent disaster, Hermione and her ladies are entertained by Mamillius's childish prattle. Leontes receives news of Camillo and Polixenes's flight, which he interprets as confirmation of his suspicions. He removes Mamillius from Hermione and accuses her publicly of adultery with Polixenes, who he claims is the father of her unborn child. She denies it, refutes his accusations with dignity and submits herself both to his commands and to the operation of heavenly providence. She and her ladies are escorted to prison, while Antigonus and other lords are left to plead on her behalf and forcibly defend her innocence. To placate them, Leontes says he has already sent Cleomenes and Dion to seek confirmation of Hermione's guilt from the oracle of Apollo at Delphos.

This is a shocking scene, which derives its power largely from Leontes's violent disruption of domestic harmony and his public shaming of his wife. It carries a similar dramatic impact to Othello's equally public humiliation of Desdemona, and removes all trace of sympathy from the king. Yet there is also an almost comic lack of authority in Leontes's failure to stifle his lords' criticisms of his actions, and Antigonus's forthrightness is the play's first real corrective to the king's increasingly deranged fantasies. His promise to 'geld' his daughters if Hermione is 'honour-flawed' is not so much a horrifying demonstration of patriarchal power as a comic hyperbole that confirms his faith in the queen. There is scope for humour, too, in the exchange between Leontes and the Lord, 'Have I done well?'; 'Well done, my lord'. Antigonus's concluding lines set the seal on Leontes's potential as comic fool, and point to an outcome which, ironically, he does not survive to witness.

In the opening section of the scene, Shakespeare deftly sketches in the secure and loving relationships centred on Hermione and Mamillius. Her pregnancy is discussed by the ladies in warmly colloquial phrases: 'The queen your mother rounds apace'; 'She is spread of late | Into a goodly bulk'. Mamillius himself is a typical Shakespearean child character, and to modern tastes he can appear irritatingly spoilt and knowing, like the doomed youngsters in other plays such as *Richard III* and *Macbeth*. His abortive story-telling, however, marks a key point in the play, invoking its title explicitly in his introductory comment, 'A sad tale's best for winter'. 'Tale' suggests something fanciful, to be taken with a pinch of salt, yet to see the whole play in this light is to diminish its essential seriousness. The reference to the season offers a good opportunity for theatrical designers to create a cold, bleak Sicilia, contrasting with the late summer setting of the Bohemian scenes, in each case matching the emotional texture of the events enacted. Mamillius does not get very far in his tale, at least as heard by the audience; but his 'sprites and goblins' are perhaps suggestive of the demons of jealousy that torment his father, whom one might identify as the man who 'dwelt by a churchyard', in the sense that he is to spend 16 years of his life visiting the chapel where lie the bodies of Mamillius himself and, as he thinks, Hermione.

Visually, this touching domestic scene continues to one side of the stage, enhancing the ominous dramatic power of Leontes's conversation with the lords on the other side, before the warm bond between mother and child is disrupted by his violent incursion, which is marked by monosyllabic brusqueness and brutally insulting language. Leontes's speeches frequently verge on incoherence, largely as a result of his exclamatory interjections and parenthetical qualifications, but his syntax here usually manages to find its way back to grammatical sense. Compared with Hermione's quiet and measured dignity, Leontes's explosive language, with its alliteration and other repetitive sound effects, suggests a mind both tortured and unbalanced. Its impact, however, is weak, not authoritative, as he perhaps realises in adopting a more controlled, if self-righteous tone in explaining that he has already sent to Apollo's oracle to confirm Hermione's guilt since, as he says with unconscious comic irony, 'in an act of this importance 'twere | Most piteous to be wild'. By the end of the scene, a number of dramatic expectations have been set up, including the tension of Hermione's imprisonment when she is so near to childbirth; the outcome of the mission to Delphos; and the speculation as to whether, in view of Hermione's belief that she is embarking on a period of suffering for her 'better grace' and Antigonus's prediction of a comic outcome, this narrative will indeed turn out to be a mere 'winter's tale'.

Act II scene 2

Prevented from speaking to the imprisoned queen in person, Paulina is allowed access to her lady, Emilia, who tells her that Hermione has given birth to a daughter. They agree that Paulina will take the child to the king in the hope that it will have a positive influence on him — an idea that Emilia says Hermione too has been toying with. The gaoler is at first reluctant to release the child, but Paulina persuades him that he has no legal reason to detain it, and promises to protect him from any repercussions.

Paulina is a striking new character: assertive, forthright, determined, resourceful and fiercely loyal to Hermione. It is worth considering why Shakespeare does not, as some directors do, introduce Paulina and Antigonus among the court attendants in Act I scene 2; and why, in this scene, he does not reveal that she is Antigonus's wife and, presumably, the mother of the three daughters he referred to in the previous scene. There is certainly a greater sense of dramatic surprise in introducing new characters only as they are needed in the action, and delaying the revelation of important information about them.

Shakespeare's treatment of the female characters is interesting, and he seems to use them both to exploit and confirm traditional female stereotypes. In the previous scene, for example, Hermione drew attention to the stereotype of the emotional woman by the very act of denying its validity in herself: 'I am not prone to weeping, as our sex | Commonly are' (II.1.108). Here, Paulina seems to present herself as another stereotype, the scold, declaring that the king 'must be told' and that 'The office | Becomes a woman best'. Her two references to her tongue confirm the convention of the nagging, shrewish woman: 'If I prove honey-mouthed, let my tongue blister', and 'I'll use that tongue I have'. Ironically, though, she also acknowledges that the image of the child itself may prove more effective, since 'The silence often of pure innocence | Persuades when speaking fails'.

Shakespeare invariably takes considerable care in creating smaller roles, and there are two typical examples in this scene. It would seem sensible to make Emilia one of Hermione's attendant ladies in the previous scene, although the text does not specify this. Like Paulina, she is loyal and protective towards the queen, and her verse is measured and dignified. There is almost a sense of a supportive sisterhood at work on Hermione's behalf, and Shakespeare imbues Emilia's language with the imagery of virtue, both homely, in terms such as 'goodly' and 'lusty'; and more abstract, in words like 'worthy', 'honour', 'goodness', 'noble' and 'blest'. There is irony in her optimism, though, which perhaps we notice even if we do not know the outcome, when Emilia tells Paulina, 'your free undertaking cannot miss | A thriving issue'. Such confidence proves to be misplaced, at least in the short term.

The gaoler, too, is deftly characterised, as a man whose moral scruples are in conflict with his job, first in admitting Paulina to the queen, which he avoids by letting her speak with Emilia, and then in allowing the baby to be taken away. He covers his back by insisting on remaining present during the women's conversation, but ultimately gives in to Paulina's 'honour' − a word spoken five times in this short scene. The gaoler is given all the characteristics of petty officialdom, in his insistence on following orders and his talk of warrants, but Shakespeare also invests him with a warm humanity – an ordinary man facing a perplexing dilemma, worried about the 'danger' he might 'incur' by breaking the rules. Appropriately, it is Paulina's telling use of legal terminology that convinces him to do the right thing, as she sets human regulations against 'the law and process of great nature', which demands the child's release. This relationship between human society and the elemental forces of Nature and Time is to become a central part of the play's abstract philosophical debate.

Act II scene 3

Racked by sleeplessness, Leontes reflects on Mamillius's sudden illness, which he blames on Hermione's shameful behaviour. He believes that only the queen's death will restore his peace of mind, but defers his thoughts of revenge against Polixenes, whom he says is too powerful. Paulina, with the baby, forces her way into the chamber despite the protestations of the lords, including her husband, Antigonus. Ignoring Leontes's commands to have her ejected, she presents the baby to him, berates him for his treatment of Hermione, refutes his protestations that he is not the child's father by drawing attention to its likeness to him, and departs, leaving the baby princess behind. Blaming Antigonus for his wife's behaviour, Leontes instructs him to see the child burned to death. Responding to the lords' pleas for mercy, however, he orders Antigonus to take the baby to some foreign shore and there abandon it. Reluctantly, and with compassion, Antigonus leaves with the child, as a servant arrives with news that Cleomenes and Dion have returned from the oracle at Delphos. Leontes orders Hermione's trial to be arranged, though to him the outcome is a foregone conclusion.

This powerful scene, centring on the confrontation between Leontes and Paulina, with the baby as its visual focus, is both serious and comic in its impact. Leontes's sleeplessness is viewed as a symptom of the disease his intemperate jealousy has brought upon himself and his son, and Paulina claims to offer him a cure as his 'physician'. These images are woven into the fabric of the language, culminating in Paulina's response to the servant who tells her that Leontes 'hath not slept tonight'. 'I come to bring him sleep,' she replies, claiming she will use 'words as med'cinal as true' that will 'purge him of that humour | That presses him from sleep'. Shakespeare had used similar imagery in previous plays. In both *Hamlet* and *Macbeth*, an act of regicide metaphorically spreads disease throughout the kingdoms of Denmark and Scotland; in the latter, Macbeth's sleeplessness is strongly suggestive of his guilty conscience, though there is no indication that guilt is at work in the mind of Leontes at this stage.

Leontes's treatment of Paulina in this scene continually plays on a set of contemporary misogynist stereotypes of women who step outside their subservient position in society. As Antigonus's wife, Paulina should bow to his control, so her independent

behaviour gives Leontes ample opportunity for a series of sarcastic jibes at the old lord's expense: 'Canst not rule her?' he demands, accusing him of being 'woman-tired', or hen-pecked, 'unroosted' by his wife whom he 'dreads' since she 'late hath beat her husband'. Antigonus, though, is quite happy to accept the reversed gender roles in his marriage, commenting ruefully, 'When she will take the rein, I let her run', and showing his approval of her independence by adding that 'she'll not stumble'. Much of the scene's deflationary humour comes from this relationship, and when Leontes suggests that Antigonus is 'worthy to be hanged' for his failure to keep his wife quiet, his comic response, 'Hang all the husbands | That cannot do that feat, you'll leave yourself | Hardly one subject' appeals to the audience's wry awareness of how the reality of marriage relationships frequently falls short of the conventional 'ideal' of wifely submission. Paulina's reputation in this respect evidently precedes her, and when Leontes rebukes Antigonus as she arrives, 'I charged thee that she should not come about me', his dejected afterthought, 'I knew she would', is what switches the scene into its comic mode.

However, it is Leontes, not Shakespeare, who consigns Paulina to the stereotype of the scold, through a series of insulting and derogatory phrases, some comic, some shockingly offensive, particularly when seen in the context of his repeated threats to have not just her, but his wife and baby daughter, 'given to the fire'. She is a 'mankind witch', a 'most intelligencing bawd', a 'callet | Of boundless tongue', a 'crone', 'a gross hag', as well as 'Dame Partlet' and 'Lady Margery'. Between them, these terms appeal to a range of antifeminist stereotypes which the scene as a whole challenges, since Paulina is, plainly, courageously in the right, while Leontes is accurately characterised by her as a 'tyrant' – though she cleverly avoids using the term as an explicit accusation. In appealing again to 'good goddess Nature', Paulina aligns herself with those positive forces which are promoted later in the play, as opposed to the unnaturalness of the witch or the masculine woman that Leontes would have her be.

It is, rather, Leontes who is behaving unnaturally, something that is revealed through the language he uses to refer to the child. While Paulina and the lords refer to the baby in compassionate terms as 'daughter', 'princess', 'babe', 'poor babe' or 'the innocent', Leontes repeatedly uses demeaning terms such as 'bastard', 'brat' or 'issue', consistently employing the pronoun 'it' to dehumanise the child he refuses to acknowledge as his. The fact that the stage baby would, in all probability, be a mere inanimate prop adds an intriguing level of discrepant awareness to these humanising and dehumanising terms.

Paulina demonstrates a range of qualities during the scene, including outspoken resistance to Leontes's threats to have her 'burnt', when she asserts that 'It is an heretic that makes the fire, | Not she which burns in't', and physical courage in the face of the men's weak attempts to remove her forcibly – 'I pray you do not push me'; 'What needs these hands?' She also shows skill in linguistic and emotional manipulation, in drawing attention to the baby's apparent likeness to Leontes. It is thus easy to overlook her grave error of judgement, perhaps even her moral culpability, in leaving the baby to Leontes's mercy. Although she is never blamed for this in the play's dialogue, and the actor of the role is given little opportunity to register her response to the consequences of her actions, except in her silent demeanour during Hermione's trial, an alert audience may well be left with doubts, not only about this but about her subsequent behaviour in the play.

Act III scene 1

Having returned from Delphos, Cleomenes and Dion reflect on their experiences there, and hope that the oracle will prove advantageous to Hermione.

Unnecessary to the structure of both narrative and plot, this scene is nonetheless crucial in our response to the play, offering, as it does, a breath of linguistic fresh air. The Sicilian court has become so claustrophobic, so bound up with images of disease and imprisonment, that it is a relief to sense that there is a world elsewhere, imbued with a sense of transcendent moral virtue and a power other than that of Leontes's obsessive tyranny. It needs little more than a listing of some of the scene's key adjectives – 'delicate', 'sweet', 'fertile', 'celestial', 'ceremonious', 'solemn', 'unearthly', 'rare', 'pleasant', 'fresh', and 'gracious' – to demonstrate the effect Shakespeare wants it to create.

Act III scene 2

At her trial, Hermione offers a dignified and eloquent self-defence. The oracle is opened and read: it declares Hermione innocent and condemns Leontes to live without an heir unless the lost child is found. As the king denounces the oracle, a servant enters to announce the death of Mamillius, at which the queen faints and is escorted out. Leontes is overcome with repentance, but Paulina returns to report that Hermione has also died. Leontes accepts Paulina's rebukes, asks to be shown the bodies of his queen and son, and promises daily penance at their tomb.

This scene offers a fast-moving sequence of dramatic events and unexpected reverses of fortune. Shakespeare now excludes all traces of comedy, so that the overall impact is tragic and moving. Indeed, the scene could well mark the conclusion of a short tragedy, were it not for the 'if' in the oracle's verdict that suggests further potential developments.

As he opens the trial, Leontes seems calm and controlled, and his language is formal and restrained. Revealingly, he uses the royal plural in his opening speech, to distance himself from personal responsibility and involvement, and appeals for respect by talking of his love for Hermione, his 'great grief' at the necessity of a trial, and his even-handed determination to pursue 'justice', whether represented by his wife's 'guilt or […] purgation'. It is not long before his veneer of reason and restraint breaks down, however, and by his speech at line 80 he has reverted to abuse, returning to the intemperate accusations of his jealous rage and referring to the baby once more as 'bastard' and 'brat'. When he now talks of justice, it is clear that the word, for him, represents only the proof of Hermione's guilt: 'so thou | Shalt feel our justice, in whose easiest passage | Look for no less than death'. He can afford, therefore, to respond to Hermione's placing herself under the judgement of Apollo's oracle by conceding that her request is 'altogether just'. Justice, however, is

impartial, and the 'sword of justice' on which Cleomenes and Dion are made to swear falls on Leontes when the oracle declares Hermione, Polixenes and Camillo to be innocent. The concept is complicated, though, by the fact that Leontes's punishment is marked by the entirely unjust deaths visited upon his son and, as it appears, his wife. Unjust actions such as his, Shakespeare seems to be suggesting, have repercussions on the guilty and the innocent alike.

During her trial, Hermione is an impressive figure on stage, whether she is made to appear upright and queenly or, ravaged by her imprisonment, weak and hardly able to stand. It is the eloquence of her language that invests her with nobility and dignity. Gone is the light wit and wordplay of her first appearance, to be replaced by a clear, straight-forward series of statements, avoiding self-pity but not excluding anger and bitterness. Unlike Leontes, she does not take refuge in the royal plural, but centres her argument around the singular personal pronoun and its variants – 'I', 'me', 'my', 'mine' – since it is her own 'integrity' that is under attack. She opens by stating her essential difficulty: nothing she can say in her defence will be believed since the entire proceedings represent a withdrawal of belief in her; thus, 'mine integrity, | Being counted falsehood, shall, as I express it, | Be so received'. She confines herself largely to the statement of known facts: her previously acknowledged virtue, her present unhappiness, the shame of her public trial. But she adds to this a faith in 'powers divine', a courageous attack on 'tyranny', an assertion that she prizes her honour above her life, and a simple denial of any dishonourable behaviour. She reminds Leontes that he himself had demanded that she show love to Polixenes, and expresses bafflement at Camillo's motive for leaving the court. In a moving conclusion to her argument, she welcomes the prospect of death, since everything that made her life worth living has been removed from her: Leontes's love, their son, their daughter and her honourable reputation. With bitter resignation she sums up, 'Tell me what blessings I have here alive | That I should fear to die'. In a series of wonderfully humanising touches, Shakespeare allows her both a powerful condemnation of the trial as 'rigour and not law' and, as a touching afterthought, an unexpected reference to her late father, the Emperor of Russia, who cannot be present to comfort her with his 'pity'.

The turning point of the scene comes with the reading of the oracle, Leontes's denunciation of it, the immediate announcement of Mamillius's death, the king's sudden repentance, and the removal of the swooning Hermione. All of this happens within 25 lines of spoken text, and shows Shakespeare to be fully in control of dramatic rhythm as he follows the tension of extended verbal discourse with a swift burst of stage action that moves the plot in a shocking and unexpected direction. Directors often enhance Shakespeare's effects in this sequence, notably by making the opening of the oracle into an impressive ritual ceremony, and by accompanying Leontes's denunciation of it with a thunderclap that not only highlights the shock of Mamillius's death but provides a prelude for the storm that is to shake the Bohemian coast in the next scene.

While Leontes's denunciation of the oracle is predictable, his subsequent change of heart is a complete surprise. His jealousy vanishes as suddenly as it arose, almost as if he has been in a temporary state of demonic possession. Perhaps aware that such a sudden reversal might seem ludicrous, Shakespeare cleverly distracts attention from it by placing Hermione's swooning and removal at exactly this point; by the time she has been taken offstage, we are somehow more prepared to accept Leontes's public speech of apology, confession and repentance at face value. In staging this, the reactions of the lords and servants are a crucial factor in guiding and shaping the response of the audience.

The scene's final shock is still to come, however, with the entrance of Paulina and her revelation of Hermione's death — a revelation that she delays until the end of a 28-line speech of passionate recrimination to Leontes for his previous actions. This is a powerful piece of rhetoric, quite different in tone from Hermione's speeches earlier in the scene. Paulina is bitter, accusing, sarcastic, insulting and deeply emotional. The rhetoric is also manipulative, aimed at creating the strongest possible abhorrence for Leontes's deeds and the most powerful emotional shock at Hermione's death, as well as testing Leontes's response to her outspokenness. As she continues, she is playing a dangerous game in calling him a tyrant and urging him, since repentance is pointless, to despair. However, in a striking change from his previous attitude to her 'boundless tongue' (II.3.91), he now tells her, 'Thou canst not speak too much'. Her risky rhetoric has proved the genuineness of his guilty sorrow, which was presumably part of her intention, and it is left to the Lord to rebuke her for overstepping the mark.

Shakespeare too is playing a dangerous game, and the actor of Paulina has a difficult decision to make. Hermione, as we learn in the play's final scene, is not dead at all, and Paulina's speech therefore represents a consummately acted performance, notably at that tricky moment when she offers to let the lords view Hermione's body. It is vital, though, that the actor plays this scene for real, giving no sense that Paulina is engaged in an elaborate moral con-trick, for the audience must believe in Hermione's death as strongly as Leontes and his court if the play's denouement is to work its dramatic magic.

Convinced of the genuineness of Leontes's repentance, Paulina apologises for her outspokenness while continuing to manipulate his feelings with rhetorical devices — notably *occupatio*, in which she manages to mention his dead queen and children and her own lost husband in the very act of saying that she will not do so. Elsewhere, this would be comic; here, it is touching. Leontes's closing speech is the clearest and simplest he has uttered so far in the play and, like him, we anticipate a long and painful process in which the daily 'recreation', or pastime, of visiting the bodies of his wife and son, will lead to his moral and spiritual re-creation. Quite what Paulina is going to show him as she leads him off to view the bodies is a question we never think to ask in looking back on this moment from the vantage point of the play's conclusion; this is, after all, a fairy tale.

Act III scene 3

Antigonus has landed on the stormy Bohemian coast, where he has decided to leave the baby, following a dream in which Hermione told him to do so. Naming the child 'Perdita' — the lost one — on Hermione's ghostly instructions, he interprets his

dream as confirmation of her guilt and Polixenes's paternity. Placing the baby on the ground with a box and papers, he flees from a pursuing bear as the storm worsens. A Shepherd in search of two missing sheep finds the child, and his son enters to report the simultaneous sinking of the ship and killing of Antigonus by the bear. Opening the box, they discover gold, causing the Shepherd to lose interest in his missing sheep. As he leaves with the child, his son goes off to bury Antigonus's remains.

Storms in Shakespeare are invariably symbolic of social and political disturbance, violence and bloodshed, while ghostly dreams and visions mark a moment of personal crisis for the characters who experience them. Both of these emblematic modes operate in the opening section of this scene. The abandonment of Perdita is not merely a pitiful human tragedy; it leaves the Sicilian throne without an heir, a situation that could lead, as Shakespeare's Jacobean audience knew only too well, to political instability and factionalism. On the individual level, however, it is a moral crime, and Antigonus and the mariners are punished by death for their complicity in it. It is pointless to consider what alternative course Antigonus could have pursued: Shakespeare simply shows that he exercises as much practical compassion as is compatible with loyal obedience to Leontes's orders. His dream, though, is intriguing.

Belief about ghosts was inconsistent in Shakespeare's time: to some they represented the genuine spirits of the dead; for others they were false apparitions adopted by evil spirits for the purpose of enticing the unwary into damnation. Antigonus admits that his dream has confuted his previous scepticism on the subject, and he interprets it as a genuine visitation from the ghost of Hermione, who must therefore be dead since apparitions of the living were rare and usually deemed impossible. It seems, then, that Shakespeare wants to reinforce the audience's belief in Hermione's death; only in retrospect might we wonder what the dream actually represented, since it turns out that Hermione was not dead after all. Much odder is the further conclusion Antigonus draws – that if Hermione is dead she must have been executed after having been proved guilty of adultery by the oracle. This provides him with a convenient explanation for the ghost's choice of Bohemia as a suitable place to leave the baby, but it also, disconcertingly, undermines his hitherto unshakeable faith in Hermione's innocence, despite the ghost's 'pure white robes, | Like very sanctity'. Strangest of all, however, is the language in which he describes the apparition – its unnerving movements and gestures, its 'gasping' prelude, its spouting eyes, and the shrieks accompanying its disappearance. Nothing could be further from the dignified human Hermione we have seen, though the ghost's speech, fortunately, offers a more measured, less melodramatically Gothic reflection of her character.

The death of Antigonus, marked by that most famous of all Shakespearean stage directions, '*Exit, pursued by a bear*', is the play's fulcrum, marking its change of mode from tragedy to comedy. The moment itself, though, has proved controversial. Is the bear's appearance in itself comic, or should the laughter begin only with the arrival of the Shepherd?

We have no way of knowing Shakespeare's intentions, nor how the bear was presented in the first productions at the Globe or the Blackfriars. Modern stagings have taken a variety of decisions, with bears ranging from the ludicrous to the terrifying, from the symbolic to the realistic, from the solidly visible to the eerily suggestive. Even bears presented seriously often raise a laugh; it seems there is something in the quality of this dramatic moment that, however it is staged, tends to prick the bubble of tension and tragedy.

What is not in doubt, is the relaxation into comedy with the arrival of the Shepherd; the transformation from courtly drama to rustic humour is reflected in the linguistic shift from blank verse to colloquial prose. Shakespeare does not patronise this Shepherd as a rustic stereotype, however; his humour derives from his knowing, worldly-wise commentary on contemporary life, from the indolence and irresponsibility of the young to the consequences of illicit sexual relations. He is also a working man whose livelihood is threatened by the loss of 'two of [his] best sheep', which have been frightened off by the activities of irresponsible young huntsmen. His reaction on discovering the baby Perdita is down-to-earth and compassionate, but not sentimental.

His son, however, is a different matter. The text designates him as 'Clown', a term that is problematic in view of the change in its meaning and associations since Shakespeare's time – an issue explored in the section on characters and characterisation (see pages 75–76). His account of the shipwreck and the death of Antigonus, switching from one to the other in his eagerness to describe both, transforms tragedy into comedy, yet avoids being distasteful by the sense of awe and wonder, mingled with simple compassion, underlying the excited confusion of the language. The Clown's respect for the victims of this dual disaster is demonstrated in his intention of burying Antigonus's remains, despite the fact that his and his father's lives have just been transformed by the discovery of the 'fairy gold'.

There is considerable scope for the actors to develop the comedy of this scene, yet it should always remain rooted in the characters as defined by the words they speak. For example, the Shepherd's apparent unwillingness to open the box himself, constantly urging his son to do it – 'Take up, take up, boy; open't. So; let's see. […] Open't. What's within, boy?' – suggests a nervousness about what it might contain that is both funny and very human. Having realised their new-found wealth, there is real comic potential in his sudden abandonment of the prize sheep he had been so eager to find: 'Let my sheep go'. This is gentle, character-based comedy and, as a result, Shakespeare is able to retain an essential thematic seriousness, granting the Shepherd what many critics see as one of the play's key symbolic lines, 'Thou met'st with things dying, I with things new born'. As the emblematic turning-point of the play, this line emphasises the transition from tragedy to comedy, from court to country, from repressive tyranny to open-hearted celebration, and paves the way for the emotional and spiritual rebirth of Leontes and the apparently physical resurrection of his queen. Modern productions almost invariably take their interval at the close of this scene.

(See also sample essay 2 (pages 127–28), which offers a close analysis of the Shepherd's first speech.)

Act IV scene 1

Time moves us on 16 years, and tells us of Leontes's self-imposed confinement. He speaks of Perdita's having grown up as the Shepherd's daughter, and mentions Polixenes's son, whom he now names as Florizel. He coyly promises that events relating to Perdita will be unfolded in due course.

A number of traditions of early modern drama come together in Shakespeare's use of Time to begin the play's second movement. As the personification of an abstract concept, he is a reminder of the old morality plays, in which such 'characters' enacted the moral and spiritual dilemmas of human existence. Roughly 15 years previously, Shakespeare had used a similar figure, Rumour, as the Prologue to *Henry IV, Part 2*, and other dramatists were still occasionally exploiting such devices. Somewhat in the manner of the morality plays, Time embodies a thematic concept, making us aware not only of the temporal context of human existence, but suggesting that time is needed for wounds to heal and the great cycles of birth, death and regeneration to take their course. In his morality guise, Time was presumably presented on stage with his traditional accoutrements of white beard, scythe, wings and hourglass – the last two of which he refers to in his speech. Perhaps he even 'flew', since actors could easily be lowered on wires from above the stage. Time's thematic control of the play is indicated in two small touches, which are easily overlooked. When he says, 'remember well | I mentioned a son o'th'king's', he is taking upon himself the role of dramatist, since Time, of course, has not previously appeared in the play, and we learned of Polixenes's son through the dialogue of Act I scene 2. And in referring to 'that wide gap', he is anticipating the play's closing speech, in which Leontes, too, refers to the 'wide gap of time' covered by the events of the play.

Time's function is also that of chorus, a dramatic device which originated in Greek tragedy as a group of actors whose communal speaking provided a commentary on the events of the play. In Elizabethan and Jacobean theatre, however, the chorus was normally a single actor whose role combined such commentary with linking narration and the establishment of a direct relationship with the audience, as well as frequently providing a prologue and/or epilogue. Shakespeare himself had often used the device, notably in *Henry V*, where the chorus is arguably the second most important character in the play, and more recently in *Pericles*, where the medieval poet Gower provides a running commentary on the events of the drama. In concluding his speech by hoping the audience members are enjoying themselves, Time is employing the kind of false modesty in drawing attention to the play as theatrical performance that was a familiar part of other Shakespearean choruses.

Another tradition of Greek drama, outlined in Aristotle's *Poetics*, is the concept of the unities, and Shakespeare blatantly draws attention to his complete disregard of these dramatic 'rules' by having Time ask us to 'Impute it not a crime | [...] that I slide | O'er sixteen years'. Though some of his contemporaries, such as Ben Jonson, advocated these classical rules of drama and criticised Shakespeare for breaking them, he rarely concerned himself with such restrictive conventions. Only in a very early play, *The Comedy of Errors*, and a very late one, *The Tempest* (possibly written immediately after *The Winter's Tale*), does he obey the unities of Time, Place and Action.

To mark out Time's role as both Chorus and allegorical morality figure, Shakespeare employs rhyming couplets – the only use of rhyme in the play except for the lyrics of the songs. Together with the rather awkwardly structured, archaic language, this creates the effect of an old-fashioned character, appropriate to Old Father Time, and lends a slightly comic edge to his appearance. In the modern theatre, his role offers a challenge, and directors have presented him in a variety of ingenious ways.

Act IV scene 2

Polixenes tries to persuade Camillo not to return to Sicilia, though Leontes has sent for him. He changes the subject to Prince Florizel's increasingly regular absences from court, and reveals that his spies have observed him visiting the home of a shepherd who has an attractive daughter and who has grown mysteriously wealthy. They decide to visit the shepherd's house in disguise to discover the reason for Florizel's visits.

Short scenes with apparently little dramatic interest can often repay close attention, and this one provides a good example since, on the face of it, it is one of the dullest parts of the play. In terms of the play's structure and the development of its story, we need to be reintroduced to Polixenes and Camillo at this point, and to learn the state of affairs in Bohemia. The scene raises immediate questions, however. Why does Shakespeare give no visible indication of the life of Polixenes's court – no lords or servants, such as those surrounding Leontes in Acts I–III; no Archidamus, whom we met at the start of the play? And why do this king and his most trusted counsellor speak in prose rather than the verse one might expect – a prose, moreover, that is flat and colourless, lacking both the exaggerated artificiality that gives energy to Camillo's and Archidamus's dialogue in I.1 and the conversation of the Gentlemen in V.2, and the colloquial vigour that enlivens the speech of Autolycus and the rustic characters?

Part of the explanation perhaps lies in the fact that we are seeing the end of a conversation – one in which Camillo has been 'importunate' in his requests to be allowed to visit Sicilia but is now forced to give up hope. There is a certain life in some of the antithetical, balanced sentences, such as Polixenes's continuation of the play's disease imagery, "Tis a sickness denying thee anything; a death to grant this'; or his poignant assertion, 'Better not to have had thee than thus to want thee'; and in the final flickers of Camillo's attempts to persuade. But as the scene turns into little more than a sharing of information about Florizel, so the style becomes dully factual: 'it is three days since I saw the prince'; 'he is seldom from the house of a most homely shepherd'; 'We must disguise ourselves'. There

is none of the richness of imagery found elsewhere in the play: Perdita is 'of most rare note' and 'the angle that plucks' Florizel to the Shepherd's cottage; otherwise the situation is explained with surprising literalness.

We are, however, given something of an insight into the workings of Polixenes's court, even though, perhaps because all available actors are preparing themselves for the sheep-shearing scene, we never see it in action. Camillo has made the mistake of becoming indispensable to the running of state affairs, having, says Polixenes, 'made me businesses which none without thee can sufficiently manage'. It appears, however, that even Camillo is not fully aware of the extent of the king's intelligence service, of which he has to be told. 'I have eyes under my service […] from whom I have this intelligence', Polixenes informs him, emphasising later, 'That's likewise part of my intelligence'. How are we meant to respond to a king who has his own son spied on?

Perhaps this merely goes with his selfishness in denying Camillo's request to return to Sicilia, which can only be excused by the lingering effects of his experience there 16 years previously. To Polixenes it is a 'fatal country', the memory of which 'punishes' him. He casts doubt on Leontes's penitence, and laments the deaths of Hermione and Mamillius 'afresh'. His sudden changing of the subject to the activities of Florizel effectively cuts off all further discussion of Camillo's request.

However, Polixenes's dwelling on the past and the intriguing undercurrents of courtly espionage are not enough to give much dramatic life to the scene, which is lacking in real tension or conflict, its main purpose being to bring us up to date as briskly as possible and prepare us for future developments. Shakespeare, however, knows his craft. By making the opening of the second part of the play so flat and undramatic, he is simply enhancing the impact of Autolycus's vivid eruption into the action and the vigour and energy of all that follows. We respond with extra warmth to Autolycus not merely because he provides relief from the tragic intensity of the first part of the play, but because he cuts through the dull, stifling atmosphere and flat language of the preceding scene. It would be possible to enliven the conversation between Polixenes and Camillo with stage business – perhaps they could be playing chess, for example, or sharing a drink – but to do so would be a betrayal of Shakespeare's intentions. If he had wanted the scene to be tense and highly charged, he could have made it so, but it exists to serve a larger dramatic purpose.

Act IV scene 3

Autolycus enters singing, and introduces himself as a rogue and former courtier, who once served Prince Florizel. Pretending to be the victim of robbery, he picks the pockets of the Clown, who is on his way to buy provisions for his sister for the sheep-shearing feast, at which Autolycus tells us he will be present.

The entrance of Autolycus into the play represents a crucial turning-point in its mood and action. He enters singing, and it is through his songs and the impressions they create that he makes his initial impact. The songs are lively and energetic, projecting a cheerfully amoral attitude to life, telling of unrepentant thieving against a natural background of spring flowers and birdsong: 'When daffodils begin to peer'; 'With heigh the sweet birds, O how they sing!'. The songs make no secret of Autolycus's vices, talking of his 'pugging tooth' and his tinker's 'sow-skin budget', of 'tumbling in the hay' and openly acknowledging potential punishment 'in the stocks'. Such risks are a fact of his life, however, and his misfortunes elicit only the comment, 'But shall I go mourn for that, my dear?' Autolycus leaves the scene as he entered it, with a song praising the virtues of the outdoor life and 'a merry heart'.

Between his snatches of song, Autolycus addresses the audience directly, not in traditional soliloquy, but in the beguiling, button-holing manner of a stand-up comic. In less than ten lines, he gives us information about his name, his recent history ('I have served Prince Florizel [...] but now I am out of service'); his current occupation ('My traffic is sheets', 'a snapper-up of unconsidered trifles'); the source of his clothes ('with die and drab I purchased this caparison'); and his attitude to a life in which the fear of 'Gallows and knock [...], Beating and hanging', causes him to 'sleep out' all thoughts of 'the life to come'. Shakespeare's exposition here is nothing if not economical.

The relationship Autolycus thus develops with the audience is crucial in our developing response to him. It enables him to share asides with us while conning the Clown, partly implicating us in his actions. When he returns to addressing the audience directly after the Clown's exit, he can tell us what he intends to do next, planting in our minds the expectation of seeing him in action again at the sheep-shearing.

Stage action is in fact one of the principal devices Shakespeare uses to present Autolycus. In this scene we have no sooner discovered how he makes his living than we see him practising his skills on the hapless Clown. Adopting a vocal disguise as a gentleman who has been mugged and robbed and his clothes exchanged with those of his assailant, he also shows us his acting skill in his piteous moaning and his dexterity in picking the Clown's pockets. Much can be made out of this in performance, and the absence of stage directions in the original Folio text leaves it open for the actors to develop their own elaborate comic business. The humour of the episode is linguistic as much as physical, however, with Autolycus's exaggerated politeness ('sweet sir', 'good-faced sir'); his relish of the portrait he paints of his own character, in the guise of describing his attacker; and the comically ironic double meanings implicit in statements such as 'Offer me no money, I pray you', thus avoiding the Clown's finding out that he no longer has any, and 'he, sir, he: that's the rogue that put me into this apparel' – a statement that is no more than the truth. The scene between Autolycus and the Clown works as a kind of double act, with the straight man's dull stupidity acting as a foil to the sharp intelligence of his comic partner.

Shakespeare also characterises Autolycus through the quality of his colloquial prose speech. He is eloquent and articulate, with a powerful command of rhetorical devices such as balanced, often antithetical sentences. His wit frequently emerges in vivid metaphorical language and wordplay, as in 'Your purse is not hot enough to purchase your spice',

or 'If the springe hold, the cock's mine'. Yet his vocabulary is rooted in everyday life, with talk of sheets, bailiffs, tinkers, puppet shows and bear-baitings. The imagery of his songs, however, lifts our appreciation of his character to another level. Though still harping on the ordinary life of 'the doxy' or the enjoyment of 'a quart of ale', the vocabulary of the songs is set against the evocation of a rural landscape of birds and flowers, haystacks and moonlit nights, footpaths and stiles.

While this language prepares us for the subsequent pastoral scenes, Shakespeare also invites us to consider a more symbolic function for this new character who, in a play entitled *The Winter's Tale*, sings of 'summer songs' and asserts that 'the red blood reigns in the winter's pale'. The positive associations of 'red blood' may remind us of Paulina's 'red-looked anger' (II.2.34) and anticipate Florizel's injunction, 'let's be red with mirth' (IV.4.54), contrasted, perhaps, with the pallor of Mamillius's cheeks as he 'declined, drooped, […] languished' (II.3.14 and 17). 'Pale', in its other sense, may suggest the constricting boundaries of the moral kingdoms over which Leontes and Polixenes 'reign', the one destroyed by his own jealousy, the other last seen planning to spy further on the activities of his son. In the play's imaginative world, these wintry realms are now usurped by the life-enhancing spirit of Autolycus's eruption into the action.

The Clown's role in the scene should not be neglected, however. His simplicity is demonstrated by his difficulties in working out the projected profit from the sheep-shearing and his gullibility in being robbed by Autolycus without even realising it. His enthusiasm for the forthcoming festivities is attractive and infectious, yet although he is likeable, our sympathy for him is outweighed by our admiration for Autolycus's consummate trickery. At the end of the scene, we eagerly anticipate the next encounter between these different types of comic character.

Act IV scene 4

Florizel and Perdita discuss their love for one another. She, dressed as queen of the feast, is apprehensive about the consequences of their relationship; he, disguised as a shepherd, Doricles, is more confident. The Shepherd enters with the Clown, the disguised Polixenes and Camillo, and all the other guests. He chides Perdita for her shyness, and recalls how his wife used to behave at such celebrations. Perdita welcomes the visitors and gives them flowers, engaging with Polixenes in a discussion on the art of grafting. She wishes she had spring flowers appropriate for the shepherdesses and for Florizel; as he praises her qualities, Polixenes and Camillo note something about her that lifts her above her station in life, and during the dance that follows, Polixenes asks the Shepherd about Florizel. The Shepherd gives his opinion that the young couple love each other equally.

The Shepherd's servant announces the arrival of a pedlar and ballad-monger, who turns out to be the disguised Autolycus. Mopsa and Dorcas, who are rivals for the Clown's affections, join Autolycus in the singing of a ballad appropriate to their situation. Further entertainment is provided by a satyr-dance performed by a company of twelve rural workers.

After the dance, Polixenes engages Florizel in conversation about his feelings towards Perdita, since he has bought her no gifts from the pedlar, and pushes him into a declaration of his love for her. Perdita echoes his feelings and the Shepherd expresses approval of their match, but Polixenes argues that Florizel's father should be consulted, drawing an irritable response from the prince. Polixenes reveals his true identity and issues a series of angry threats: he will disinherit his son and subject Perdita to torture and death if they continue to see each other; while the Shepherd, first threatened with death, will suffer only the king's displeasure. On Polixenes's departure, the lovers assess the situation, while the Shepherd bemoans his fate and casts blame on Perdita for knowingly consorting with the prince. Perdita assumes their relationship is over but Florizel, determined not to submit to his father, asks Camillo, whose identity he has guessed, to tell Polixenes that he and his mistress have set sail for an undisclosed destination. Seeing an opportunity to fulfil his own wish to return to Sicilia, Camillo suggests that they should visit Leontes there, on the pretext of a diplomatic mission, while he tries to talk Polixenes into accepting their union. Florizel agrees, but points out that his princely status will be questioned since he is dressed as a shepherd.

While Florizel discusses practicalities with Camillo, Autolycus returns, gloating over the profit he has made, not only from the sale of his trinkets but from his pickpocketing exploits, which were unfortunately cut short by the distressed Shepherd's interruption of the proceedings. Camillo gives Autolycus money to change clothes with Florizel, while Perdita is to wear Florizel's hat, so that they can reach the ship undetected. Camillo's intention is to tell the king where the lovers have fled, so that, accompanying him in his pursuit of them, he will be able to return to Sicilia. Having grasped the essence of what is going on, Autolycus decides not to tell the king about it, since it is more in keeping with his knavery to support Florizel's deception. He accosts the Shepherd and Clown, who are anxiously debating the wisdom of telling the king the truth about Perdita's origins, to absolve themselves of blame; they decide to prove their story by presenting Polixenes with the items that were found with her, which they have in a bundle, together with the original box. Removing his false beard and pretending to be a courtier, Autolycus interrogates them about the contents of the box and bundle, tells them they cannot see the king at the palace because he has gone on board his new ship, and terrifies them with the prospect of the dreadful tortures that lie in store for them, while pretending not to know who they are. He agrees, though, to escort them to the king, for which they pay him gold, promising more later. In reality, Autolycus intends to take them to Florizel's ship, hoping for further rewards from the prince.

This long scene is structured essentially as a sequential narrative, forming an interesting contrast to the scene of the Capulets' ball in *Romeo and Juliet*, where there is a more complex interlocking structure to the various narrative threads. Shakespeare begins by introducing us to the final pair of new characters, Florizel and Perdita, whose relationship is central to the remainder of the play. Both are strongly characterised, yet modern actors often have difficulty in bringing them to life with conviction and credibility: as a romantic couple, they can seem flat and colourless stereotypes, he callow and slightly pompous, she rather prim and sentimental. There are various reasons for this, relating partly to the difference in linguistic conventions associated with romantic love. From the start of the scene, there is a clear contrast in their characters and their attitudes to their situation. Both are dressed up in costumes that reverse their social status: Perdita as queen of the feast, Florizel as a shepherd. Florizel revels in these transformations, suggesting that her 'unusual weeds […] give a life' to each part of her, and equating himself with those gods who transformed themselves into lesser creatures – bull, ram and 'poor humble swain' – for the sake of love. Perdita, though, is uneasy about her dressing up and his disguise: he is 'obscured | With a swain's wearing' and she 'most goddess-like pranked up', which would cause her, in normal circumstances, to 'blush | To see [him] so attired' or 'swoon' to look at her own reflection. For her, his nobility is 'vilely bound up' in his shepherd's clothes, while her regal robes are 'borrowed flaunts' – the language in both phrases strongly suggesting her deep unease. Such unease is a feeling that Shakespeare, in most of his plays, would share: he almost invariably associates false appearances with evil, and it is worth considering whether the scene as a whole, in which Polixenes, Camillo and Autolycus are also in disguise, and where Florizel and Perdita change their outward appearances yet again at the end, makes any implicit moral statement on the issue.

Perdita's discomfort is closely bound up with her intense awareness of the difference in status between herself and Florizel which, as she says, 'forges dread'. This is a strong word, but her fear is palpable as she confesses, 'I tremble | To think your father […] | Should pass this way'. Florizel's response to her concerns is confident and even dismissive, with a complacency that is not particularly attractive in its apparent absence of sympathetic understanding. All he can do is offer a series of instructions to her, expressed in the imperative: 'Apprehend nothing but jollity', 'darken not | The mirth o'th'feast', 'Be merry', 'Strangle such thoughts as these', 'Lift up your countenance', 'Address yourself to entertain them sprightly'. Although in these commands he is in tune with the celebratory atmosphere of this section of the play, concluding 'let's be red with mirth', his insistence suggests a shallow understanding of the reality of their situation. However, his evident love for Perdita is strongly expressed, and he impressively distances himself from accusations of merely physical infatuation through the strength of his comment, 'my desires | Run not before mine honour, nor my lusts | Burn hotter than my faith'.

Perdita's unwillingness to play a role is made evident in her initial reluctance to enter into the spirit of the festivities, causing the Shepherd to contrast her 'retired' demeanour with the energetic hospitality offered by his late wife and demanding that she 'quench [her] blushes'. To the Shepherd, her role as 'Mistress o'th'Feast' is not a performance; it is, he tells her, 'that which you are'. She remains uneasy, however, and aware of the power of acting to reshape reality, as is made clear by her comment:

> Methinks I play as I have seen them do
> In Whitsun pastorals; sure this robe of mine
> Does change my disposition.

When circumstances change, she is only too eager to discard what she sees as her artificial self: 'I'll queen it no inch farther'; she remains reluctant to adopt disguises, even out of necessity, later in the scene, when she says, 'I see the play so lies | That I must bear a part'. Sensing her unease, Camillo firmly responds, 'No remedy'.

It is in her distribution of flowers to the assembled company that Perdita's role in the scene reaches its height. Combining the flower imagery itself with references to the seasons, her language embodies some of the play's central issues, with the inexorable cycle of life seen symbolically under the control of 'great creating nature'. Her choice of flowers is limited by the season; as she says, the year is 'growing ancient, | Not yet on summer's death nor on the birth | Of trembling winter'. Yet despite the consequent unavailability of spring flowers appropriate to the younger members of the company, she is able to conjure them up in some of the most vivid and beautiful language of the play. To modern sensibilities, these flower speeches may seem to make her romantically sentimental, but looked at more closely the language is often expressive of strength and power, as with the daffodils that 'come before the swallow dares, and take | The winds of March with beauty'. 'Take' literally means to enchant — itself a much stronger verb in Shakespeare's time than it has since become, suggestive of a hypnotic magical power. But it also implies that the daffodils vigorously enjoy the winds' strength, or even take control of it, and the verb has sexual connotations too. The daffodils here are not the sentimentalised flowers of modern greetings card verses, but vibrant and vigorous manifestations of natural beauty — more courageous than the swallow, suggests Perdita, in braving the boisterous March winds. Such qualities thus attach themselves to Perdita too, when the winds of Polixenes's wrath fail to shake her determination: 'I was not much afeard,' she says:

> for once or twice
> I was about to speak and tell him plainly
> The self-same sun that shines upon his court
> Hides not his visage from our cottage but
> Looks on alike.

In these lines, she seems to be promoting a kind of humane social equality, despite her earlier unhappiness with the difference in status between herself and Florizel; her moral

courage continues when she later asserts, 'I think affliction may subdue the cheek, | But not take in the mind'. Yet Perdita does not actually respond in the face of Polixenes's angry threats, and she is largely silent during the remainder of the scene, speaking barely 20 lines out of the 218 that remain before she, Florizel and Camillo exit. It is almost as if Shakespeare reduces her status to the feminine stereotype of silent victimhood, emphasised by her determination to 'milk [her] ewes, and weep'.

Central to our impression of Perdita in this scene is her debate with Polixenes on the subject of grafting, in which the relative merits of 'art' and 'nature' are held up for examination. Art stands here for any human interference in the workings of the natural world, and the debate, though in many ways it seems dramatically irrelevant, was an important one for the Jacobeans. If we realise that the same debate remains a hot topic today, not only in the controversy over natural and artificial food production techniques, or food additives, or building materials, but shifted by scientific advances into the areas of genetic engineering, cloning, transplant surgery and stem cell research, perhaps the discussion becomes more vivid for us. More importantly, it widens our response to the characters. Perdita objects to growing 'carnations' and 'gillyvors' because they are not natural, but the artificial products of grafting and cross-breeding. Polixenes argues that all such activities are natural, because the humans who carry them out are themselves part of nature, so that 'over that art, | Which […] adds to nature, is an art | That nature makes' – thus, 'the art itself is nature'. Perdita is forced to admit he is right – 'so it is' – but stubbornly refuses to change her initial conviction.

The debate is deepened for the audience by the various levels of irony that underlie it, in which the two debaters essentially argue for a position on the issue of grafting which is opposite to that they adopt on the level of personal and social relationships. Polixenes may advocate 'marry[ing] | A gentler scion to the wildest stock, | [To] make conceive a bark of baser kind | By bud of nobler race', but will not countenance such interbreeding in the case of his son and a shepherdess. Perdita, conversely, objects to such interbreeding in botany, but is herself engaged in it on the human level. The complex irony is deepened by the audience's awareness that she is not in fact a shepherdess at all, but a princess, and that Polixenes's true 'nature' is concealed by the 'art' of disguise. Trying to extract Shakespeare's own viewpoint out of all this is, as so often, both impossible and pointless. However, the debate does seem to invest Perdita with an element of primness that is confirmed when she orders the servant to 'forewarn' the approaching pedlar 'that he use no scurrilous words in's tunes'.

Florizel also demonstrates a mixture of attractive and unattractive qualities. He expresses his love for Perdita in beautiful and lyrical language when he addresses her directly, notably in his speech beginning, 'What you do | Still betters what is done', its rhythms and onomatopoeic effects gently reflecting the 'wave o'th'sea' to which he likens her; and with forceful sincerity when he is pushed by Polixenes into a public defence of his feelings for her, asserting that he 'would not prize' any worldly accomplishments 'without her love'. Yet he can also seem pompous, self-righteous and arrogant, particularly in his discussion with the 'ancient sir' whom he fails to recognise as his father, whose views he dismisses with discourteous contempt:

> I yield all this;
> But for some other reasons, my grave sir,
> Which 'tis not fit you know, I not acquaint
> My father of this business.

There is something callous, too, in his reference to his father's prospective death:

> One being dead,
> I shall have more than you can dream of yet.

Florizel comes across much more sympathetically in his conversation with Camillo after the king's departure. His language is infused with love, sincerity and strength of purpose, and while his own plans are rash and impulsive, he submits himself with respect and sensitivity to Camillo's guidance. Shakespeare allows him a range of powerful images that add both strength and depth to his character, as when he calls on nature to 'crush the sides o'th'earth together | And mar the seeds within' if he should ever violate his faith. Such language is redolent of Shakespeare's great tragic heroes such as Macbeth and King Lear.

There is, then, a great deal of scope for actors to create complex and interesting characters out of Florizel and Perdita, and it is curious that they so often seem rather pale and lifeless in modern performances. Perhaps one problem is that they have to strive to make an impact against the celebratory noise and physicality of the sheep-shearing festivities. When the scene is allowed to turn, as it so often does, into a full-scale piece of musical theatre, Florizel and Perdita can fight a losing battle for the audience's attention. In 1969, Trevor Nunn staged it along the lines of the hippy 'love-rock musical', *Hair*; Nicholas Hytner in 2001 turned it into the Glastonbury Festival; and in 2002 Matthew Warchus gave it the feel of Rodgers and Hammerstein's *Oklahoma!* In all three versions, Autolycus became the star of the show, and his activities, roguish but life-enhancing, were central to the symbolic impact of the Bohemian scenes. Despite Perdita's warnings about scurrility, there is a great deal that is both earthy and bawdy in the scene, from the suggestive account the servant gives of Autolycus's 'love-songs', with their lyrics of 'jump her and thump her', which perhaps motivate Perdita's attempt at censorship, to the dance of the satyrs, traditionally represented as half-goat, half-man, with enormous erect phalluses — something of an embarrassment to Perdita, one assumes. By the end of the scene, though, Autolycus's dramatic impact is diminished as he becomes reduced to a mere pawn in the escape plans of Florizel and Perdita, though his encounter with the Shepherd and Clown restores him to a certain level of comic authority.

There is only space here for a brief mention of the other elements of the scene. The Shepherd and Clown are treated with great respect by Shakespeare, without a hint of condescension. The father is dignified by formal blank verse culminating in a moving

outburst of grief and despair. His son is given an attractively enthusiastic simplicity, and deals sensitively with the rivalry of Mopsa and Dorcas for his affections. To some extent, they lose these qualities in their dialogue with Autolycus, in which they are transformed into rather gormless comic dupes, with the Shepherd reverting to prose. Shakespeare can afford to diminish their status here, though, knowing that they will turn the tables on Autolycus by the end of the play.

Polixenes and Camillo arouse mixed responses in the scene. Their impact also depends on the kind of disguises they are given which, in some productions, can make them seem rather comic at first. At the start, Polixenes seems reasonable, and he is impressed by Perdita's poise and beauty, as is Camillo, recognising that 'Nothing she does or seems | But smacks of something greater than herself, | Too noble for this place'. He gives ample opportunity for Florizel to take a different course of action in pursuing his love, but his apparent reasonableness is shattered by the violence of his anger and the cruelty of his threats when he reveals his true identity. It is instructive to compare his role here with that of Leontes in the first part of the play; if he seems a less powerful character, that simply reflects the different nature of his passionate feelings and the different context in which they are displayed. As the father furious with his child's independence in choosing relationships, he is partly a familiar stereotype that runs through Shakespeare's drama from Egeus in *A Midsummer Night's Dream* and Capulet in *Romeo and Juliet* to the king in *Cymbeline*. Camillo, meanwhile, is a more transparent character, amusingly so in his admiration of Perdita, with whom he flirts wittily in his comment, 'I should leave grazing, were I of your flock, | And only live by gazing'. He retains his disguise after Polixenes has revealed himself, and his remaining behind when his master sweeps out suggests a certain disapproval of the king's behaviour that is similar to his response to Leontes's jealousy in Act I. There is a comic moment when, having offered advice to Florizel with his disguise still in place, the prince has to confirm his identity – 'I think, Camillo?' – at which he presumably removes it. But there are selfish reasons behind Camillo's helping of the lovers, and there is a sense in which he underplays the dangers and uncertainties of the course he advises them to take, in order to have a chance of achieving his desire to revisit Sicilia, which he shares with the audience in two rather clumsy asides as Florizel and Perdita talk apart (Lines 486–92 and 631–36). Camillo should nevertheless remain an honest character, motivated largely by loyalty and sympathy, and it is clear that he will pursue his own ends only in the context of working towards the reconciliation of Polixenes and Florizel, and promoting the union of the prince and Perdita. In imagery typical of the play, Florizel appropriately calls him 'the medicine of our house'.

One final element of the scene that is worthy of comment relates to the exchange of clothes between Florizel and Autolycus. The practical stage business of this is easy enough, but there is a problem for the costume designer. Essentially, the clothes that have made Florizel look like a shepherd must make Autolycus look like a courtier – an apparently impossible feat. In fact, the exchange invariably works in the theatre without our noticing anything anomalous, and the key lies in Autolycus's performance. It is the power of his acting (as well as his removal of the pedlar's false beard) that must convince the Shepherd and Clown of his courtly status, as well as ensuring that they fail to recognise him from their previous encounters. The Shepherd does, in fact, comment on his clothes: 'His garments are rich, but he wears them not handsomely'; we just have to accept that, perhaps because of his distracted state, this is how he sees Autolycus, and that he is led to such an assessment by his courtly voice, posture and body language. Why he fails to recognise the clothes as those worn earlier by Florizel is just one of those questions that, in the theatre, we don't ask. The convention of disguises is that we are required to accept the impression they make on others. It is the laws of drama that apply, not those of realistic logic.

Act V scene 1

The action returns to Sicilia, where Cleomenes and Dion attempt to persuade Leontes that he has performed more than ample penance for his sins, and urge him to consider remarriage in order to provide the kingdom with an heir. Paulina opposes them, however, and Leontes promises not to take a new wife without her permission — which she says she will only give when Hermione is restored to life. A servant announces the unexpected arrival of Florizel and his princess, and Leontes welcomes the visitors, in whom he sees the image of his lost son and daughter. Florizel offers greetings from Polixenes, and claims that Perdita is a Libyan princess whom he has married. A lord announces Polixenes's arrival in Sicilia with the revelation that Perdita is a mere shepherd's daughter, and that she and Florizel should be apprehended. The Shepherd and Clown have also arrived in Sicilia, and Polixenes has threatened to torture them to death. Florizel assumes he and Perdita have been betrayed by Camillo, who is with Polixenes, and confesses that they are not married. Leontes, expressing admiration for Perdita's beauty despite her lowly status, agrees to act as an advocate for the young lovers with Polixenes.

Shakespeare's first concern in this scene is to show the changes that have taken place in Leontes since the start of the play. Sixteen years of penance have transformed him from a volatile, unstable tyrant, subject to paranoid delusions, into a calm, reflective recluse, unable to forget the wife and children destroyed by his own intemperate actions. These changes are made explicit in every aspect of his language, from the evenness of its verse rhythms to the clarity of its grammatical structures and the quality of its imagery. He is entirely under the influence of Paulina who, with her usual sharpness, takes every opportunity to remind him of what he has destroyed. Leontes's inertia and Paulina's controlling influence are creating increasingly urgent political anxieties for his lords, centred on the absence of an heir to the throne. As Dion argues, this may cause 'dangers' to 'drop upon his kingdom and devour | Incertain lookers-on', and the king needs to consider taking another wife. The lords' irritation with Paulina is understandable, since her own attitude to the problem of the succession seems completely inadequate, relying on the oracle's prediction that there will be no heir 'Till his lost child be found'. She asserts vaguely that

'The crown will find an heir' and cites the example of Alexander the Great, who left his kingdom 'to th'worthiest'.

With hindsight, we can see Paulina's difficulties here, and an actor in the role can build on the subtle hints that Shakespeare gives of her anxieties – for, of course, unknown to the king, the lords and the audience, it is simply not possible for Leontes to remarry, since Hermione is still alive. How much desperation should be evident in Paulina's demeanour is questionable, since the play's final secret must not at this stage be hinted at, but the hope with which she and Hermione have sustained themselves, that the abandoned princess may be found, must be wearing rather thin. There should at any rate be enormous relief in her response to Leontes's promise that he will not remarry 'till thou bid'st us'.

The announcement of Florizel and Perdita's unexpected arrival provides a brilliant opportunity for the actor playing the servant who brings the news – a parallel role to the enthusiastic servant who heralds the arrival of Autolycus and later the dancers in the sheep-shearing scene. In both cases, Shakespeare takes care not to offer a dismissive or patro-nising characterisation, giving real personalities to these servants above and beyond their mechanical narrative functions. This servant echoes the previous one's enthusiasm in his account of Perdita, whose attractions he cannot stop mentioning: she is 'The fairest I have yet beheld', 'the most peerless piece of earth […] | That e'er the sun shone bright on' who would 'make proselytes | Of who she but bid follow'; 'a woman,' he concludes, 'More worth than any man' – indeed – 'The rarest of all women.' This is entertaining, particularly in view of Paulina's attempt to deflate his exaggeration, seeing it as disloyalty to the memory of Hermione, but it is also important at this stage in the play that we recognise the impact Perdita makes on others, revealing her true status as a princess. What is most intriguing about the servant, though, is how Shakespeare makes him a kind of court poet, whose previous verse in praise of Hermione had once 'Flowed with her beauty', according to Paulina. When she comments, 'your writing now | Is colder than that theme', it is not clear whether she is saying Hermione's death had already removed his inspiration and dulled his poetic skill, or whether it is his praise of Perdita that marks a diminution in his talent. Whatever the interpretation, an actor cast in this role, particularly if doubled with the Shepherd's servant, would have plenty of material on which to exercise his skill.

Florizel and Perdita have been engaged in a serious deception since their first appearance in the play, but their status as romantic lovers has somehow justified their behaviour, which in any case seems to be a purely domestic affair. In fact, Florizel's deter-mination to marry a shepherd's daughter would have severe political repercussions for the kingdom of Bohemia, particularly if Polixenes stuck to his threat to 'bar [Florizel] from succession' (IV.4.408), plunging the country into a crisis similar to that facing Sicilia. When the lovers enter the Sicilian court, though, their deception is raised to the level of interna-tional politics, and it is disconcerting to see the extent of Florizel's blatant lies as he claims to be his father's representative on a diplomatic mission, introduces Perdita as the wife he has brought from Libya and attempts to explain his lack of attendants. It is notable that Perdita herself does not speak during this sequence, and an actor must decide how much unease she should show at being central to such a tissue of fabrication. Perdita's only verbal contribution to the scene is her response to the later report of Polixenes's treatment of her father and brother, in which her anxiety for them vies with distress at the threat to her marrying Florizel. Florizel's pack of lies comes crashing around his ears, but he is able to behave with dignity in admitting the truth, asserting his unshakable love for Perdita, and asking for Leontes's help.

In this final part of the scene, Leontes himself acquires a genuine air of decisive authority – probably the first and only time in the play where we see him behaving as a king ideally should. Yet his role here, and indeed earlier in the scene, is undercut by some rather dubious remarks that impart an edgy quality to the proceedings. His initial greeting to Florizel, for example, is worthy of close examination:

> Your mother was most true to wedlock, prince,
> For she did print your royal father off,
> Conceiving you.

In view of previous events, the emphasis on Polixenes's queen evidently not having been an adulteress is distinctly crass; Leontes is clearly still obsessed with the issue of fidelity in marriage. Essentially, though, Leontes means to say nothing more than that Florizel resembles his father, a resemblance that calls up all the pain of his treatment of Polixenes. His response to Perdita is more ambiguous, however. Like the servant, he is struck by her beauty and calls her 'goddess' and 'paragon', and it is clear that she makes him think of both his wife and his own lost daughter: twice he imagines that in looking at Florizel and Perdita he might be looking at his own children (lines 131–33, 175–77). On learning that Perdita is no more than a shepherdess, his reaction is conventional: he is sorry she is 'not so rich in worth as beauty', as if 'worth' were a quality defined purely by social status. Almost immediately, however, he finds himself thinking of her in another way, as a potential wife for himself. If, as Florizel says, Polixenes would grant him anything, he would 'beg [Florizel's] precious mistress'. To the knowing audience, this has unfortunate suggestions of incest – something more explicitly developed in Greene's *Pandosto*. He answers Paulina's rebuke, however, by explaining that his comment was motivated solely by Perdita's resemblance to his wife. Paulina's intervention, incidentally, is her first speech since Florizel and Perdita's entrance, and she takes the opportunity to be dismissive about Perdita's attractions in comparison with Hermione. As so often, an actor must decide what has been going through her mind here: how far she too has been impressed by Perdita's likeness to Hermione, whether she begins to suspect her true identity, or whether she is genuinely offended by Leontes's unguarded remark.

The imagery of the scene is partly responsible for creating its particular atmosphere of serenity and acceptance tinged with enduring sadness and regret. Cleomenes sets the tone with the religious vocabulary of his opening speech, expressed in the Christian terminology of sin, penance and redemption. Only his reference to 'the heavens' rather than 'Heaven' reminds us that the play's action ostensibly moves in a setting of pagan theology.

Leontes, too, uses similar vocabulary, in one speech referring to Polixenes as 'holy', 'graceful', 'sacred' and 'blest', regretting the 'sin' he has committed against him, and invoking both 'the blessèd gods' and 'the heavens'. In welcoming the young lovers, Leontes also employs two of the play's other key images – the seasons and disease. In each case he sees their arrival as the opportunity for a new beginning: they come 'as […] the spring to th'earth', and he hopes that the gods will 'purge all infection' from the air during their stay. The lovers are clearly invested, through this language, with symbolic associations suggesting the power of youth to bring healing and renewal, that reverberate throughout the play.

(See also sample essay 3 (pages 128–30), which offers a comparison of one of Leontes's speeches in this scene with an earlier speech from the play.)

Act V scene 2

Autolycus learns, through the discussion of three Gentlemen, of the reunion of Leontes with Polixenes and Camillo, and the revelation of Perdita's true identity. Paulina has invited the assembled company to view the statue of Hermione that she has had made. Autolycus reflects ruefully on his unknowing role in bringing about these remarkable events. The Shepherd and Clown, revelling in their new status as gentlemen, promise to put in a good word to Florizel on Autolycus's behalf, providing he mends his ways.

If we do not know the story, we are likely to expect the play to conclude with the reunion of the two kings and the revelation that Perdita is Leontes's lost daughter. It comes as an enormous surprise, then, to find these events recounted at second hand by three brand new characters. Only when we learn of Hermione's statue does it become clear that Shakespeare has another conclusion planned: one which, despite the hints he supplies, we have little chance of predicting.

We have not heard language quite the same as the Gentlemen's courtly, artificial prose since the play's opening dialogue between Camillo and Archidamus. Its effect here is difficult to judge, and its impact on stage is often rather undramatic. There is no doubt that it is partly intended to be comic, as if the speakers are vying with each other to see who can provide the most rhetorically impressive account. Certainly, the many rhetorical devices in these speeches seem self-consciously elaborate. The persistent antithetical balance is notable, in phrases that oppose 'speech' with 'dumbness', 'language' with 'gesture' and, on three separate occasions, 'joy' with 'sorrow', as well as highlighting contrasting verbs: 'ransomed'/'destroyed'; 'seen'/'spoken of'; 'lost'/'found'; and 'declined'/'elevated'. Such antithetical structures can be more complex than a mere balancing of vocabulary, and the grammatical phrasing often has the effect of paradox, thus investing the speaker with an even greater degree of linguistic wit. Sometimes these paradoxical statements are not easy to grasp at one hearing, as in the 3rd Gentleman's comment, 'I never heard of such another encounter, which lames report to follow it and undoes description to do it'. Other examples convey their point with a more vivid if hyper-bolical impact: Perdita, says the same character, 'did [...], I would fain say bleed tears; for I am sure my heart wept blood'. Other rhetorical devices are employed too, most commonly by the 3rd Gentleman, to whom the bulk of the account belongs. He employs the listing technique in the 'proofs' of Perdita's identity, and self-consciously points up his own witty use of metaphor in remarking that Perdita's emotional response was the sight that 'angled for [his] eyes – caught the water though not the fish'. It would be possible for the wit of these characters to distract us from the story they are telling. Thus, although it must be tempting for actors to create interesting characterisations from their rather unpromising lines, they need to remember that their basic function here is to convey narrative information.

The events described by these characters are both moving and comic, emphasised by that repeated antithesis of 'joy' and 'sorrow', and it is easy to miss some striking moments in the general sense of excited wonder and linguistic display. Ballads have featured earlier in the play, often dealing with grotesque and impossible occurrences, but this event, according to the 2nd Gentleman, was so amazing 'that ballad-makers cannot be able to express it'. It is, in fact, more like 'an old tale', as both 2nd and 3rd Gentlemen describe it: something that has to be told 'though credit be asleep and not an ear open' – in other words, even though no one is likely to believe it. Perhaps the play too, as a winter's tale, is meant to be seen in this way. Yet there are more serious matters involved, such as the suggestion that 'all the instruments which aided to expose the child were even then lost when it was found', thus investing the deaths of Antigonus and the sailors with a sense of moral retribution. And there is a touching description of Leontes's moral courage in recounting to Perdita the circumstances of her mother's death: 'with the manner how she came to't bravely confessed and lamented by the king'. All this would have been dramatic material for a direct enactment of the scene, but perhaps Shakespeare thought it would detract from the impact of the surprise denouement he had planned.

The nature of this denouement is hinted at not so much in the mention of Hermione's statue, as in the 2nd Gentleman's comment that he thought Paulina 'had some great matter there in hand, for she hath privately twice or thrice a day ever since the death of Hermione visited that removed house'. Has it really taken 16 years for Julio Romano to complete his commission? We are eager to accompany the Gentlemen to see the statue and discover if indeed 'some new grace will be born'.

Shakespeare has a further purpose in this scene, namely to conclude the roles of Autolycus, the Shepherd and the Clown. Autolycus, who entered the play with such a dramatic flourish, leaves it with a distinct whimper. Not only is he denied any concluding songs, but he is sidelined by the Gentlemen's discussion and bested by his former victims, whose assistance he has to beg in restoring him to favour with Florizel. The old Autolycus would certainly be an inappropriate presence in the subdued atmosphere of the play's conclusion, but the fading out of his role is a definite anticlimax. Autolycus himself seems aware of a diminution in his status, though he does try to convince himself that he still has 'the dash of [his] former life' in him. He professes relief at having avoided being the bringer of good news, since that 'would not have relished among [his] other discredits' and he admits that he has 'done good to' the Shepherd and Clown against his will. It is not clear whether these two now know who Autolycus really is, nor whether they are fully aware of his previous contacts with them in various disguises; the Clown's reference to Autolycus's recent refusal to fight him suggests such a discovery, but it is left unexplained. It is satisfying, though, that the rustics have the upper hand, and the comedy of their naïve response to their social elevation is not without a certain dignity. It is notable that Autolycus's four responses to the Clown are brief and subservient, and he is not even allowed the last word. It is as if, uprooted from his native environment, there is no role for him in the world of Sicilia.

There is apparently no role, either, for the Shepherd and Clown in the final scene of the play. Ambiguously, the Clown refers at the end of the scene to 'the kings and princes [...] going to see the queen's picture' and invites Autolycus to follow them, but the assumption that they are going to join their new 'kindred' at this event proves to be mistaken as they are not specified as being present in the stage directions of the next scene. They may now be gentlemen, the play seems to say, but their social origins make them unworthy of a place at such a solemn ceremonial occasion which is to evoke a sense of transcendental wonder. Ignoring their textual absence, however, some productions have dignified them by allowing them to participate in the marvels of the play's conclusion.

Act V scene 3

Paulina reveals the statue of Hermione to her assembled guests. They wonder at its lifelike quality, and are powerfully moved by the feelings and memories it evokes. Paulina claims to be able to make the statue move and, as it comes to life to the sound of music, it is revealed to be the real Hermione, preserved alive with Paulina's aid in the hope that her lost daughter would one day be found. She embraces Leontes and gives Perdita her blessing. Paulina wryly acknowledges her exclusion from this reunion, since her own husband cannot be restored to her, but Leontes pairs her off with Camillo, offers a final plea to Hermione and Polixenes to forgive his jealous suspicions, and urges Paulina to lead the company away to share each other's stories.

The final scene of The Winter's Tale never fails to exert a powerful and moving effect, even in an otherwise indifferent production. In the modern theatre, even when we do not know the story, we are likely to guess the outcome as soon as we see the statue revealed, since it is usually clear that it is, in fact, the actor who played Hermione. Jacobean audiences, however, would be used to seeing statues represented on stage by real actors – presumably this saved on the expense of creating elaborate props. Thus it would be a genuine surprise when the 'statue' moved. Yet the scene does not rely on this element of surprise in creating its magical effect; after all, many of those first audiences must have revealed the ending to friends who were going to see the play, and it must have been familiar to spectators at the numerous court performances given between 1611 and 1640. So how does Shakespeare ensure that, whether we know the outcome or not, the denouement retains its sense of mystery and wonder?

The key to the scene's effect lies mostly in the careful use of Paulina as both director and stage manager of the denouement. First she builds up her visitors' anticipation by giving them a tour of the rest of her gallery before revealing the statue. She cunningly calculates its effect on them, twice warning them not to touch it because the paint is still wet (lines 47, 81–82), threatening three times to close the curtain because of the powerful emotional effect it has produced (lines 59, 68, 83), and persistently hinting at the possibility that the statue might move and even come to life (lines 60–61, 69–70, 74–75, 87–89). This piece of carefully staged theatre then reaches its climax accompanied by the dramatic use of music, as Paulina gently prompts the still Hermione into motion.

To a large extent, Shakespeare uses the reactions of Paulina's onstage spectators to guide the response of the real audience. Their sense of wonder and amazement rubs off on us, and her injunction to Leontes, 'It is required | You do awake your faith', acts also as an exhortation to us to suspend our disbelief. It is notable that, throughout this sequence, Shakespeare is at pains to reassure us that no magic or witchcraft is involved in the reanimation of Hermione – something to which a Jacobean audience would have been particularly sensitive. He does this partly through seeping the scene in the religious imagery of grace, penance, blessing and redemption, and partly by making the characters explicitly aware of the potential supernatural explanation, and having Paulina deny it. Leontes first suggests that the 'magic' of the statue has 'conjured' up the memory of his evil deeds, and has 'took the spirits' from Perdita, turning her to stone. In kneeling to the statue, Perdita herself is anxious that the onlookers should 'not say 'tis superstition', while Paulina suggests Leontes has been 'transported' and he himself talks of his 'madness' – both possible effects of magical enchantment. Thus when Paulina promises to make the statue move, she is anxious to 'protest against' the assumption that she is 'assisted | By wicked powers', and urges those who think she is engaged in 'unlawful business' to depart. As Hermione descends, Paulina reassures the company that 'her actions shall be holy as | You hear my spell is lawful'. Leontes is not quite convinced: 'If this be magic,' he says, 'let it be an art | Lawful as eating.'

Having descended from the pedestal, Hermione embraces Leontes but does not speak to him; after all, as many commentators have pointed out, what could she possibly say? Her only speech is addressed to her daughter, for whose sake, she makes it clear, she has 'preserved' herself and, using the same word, asks to hear how Perdita has been 'preserved'. Many features of her speech are puzzling. Her invocation to the gods to bless her daughter is powerful and moving, but why does she ask for the details of Perdita's history? Surely Paulina must have told her all this in preparing her for her restoration? And why does she say Paulina told her of the oracle's pronouncement, when in fact she was in court to hear it for herself, responding with the exclamation, 'Praised!' (III.2.134)? And why does Shakespeare end her speech with a pun, playing on three meanings of the word

'issue'? Its primary meaning here is simply the 'outcome' of events, but it also carries the senses of both 'child' and 'heir', used frequently during the play. It is as if the dramatist is reminding us that Sicilia now has an heir to the throne, as if this, rather than the human reunion, is the most important consequence of these remarkable events.

There are other oddities in the scene, which require careful interpretation by theatrical practitioners. Why, for example, does Polixenes rather oddly lay the blame on himself for Leontes's jealousy, calling himself 'him that was the cause of this'? And what does Leontes mean at the end by saying to Hermione, 'What! Look upon my brother'? Has he noticed that she is reluctant to look at Polixenes, and is telling her to do so, since there is now no likelihood of his misinterpreting their 'holy looks'? Or does he suddenly notice that she is looking at Polixenes, causing a brief reawakening of his old jealousy, which he hastily has to suppress in asking for their pardon? How this moment is represented on stage will depend on a director's view of the precise degree of harmony and reconciliation embodied in the happy ending. It is already crafted to contain unresolved elements of tragedy, in the deaths of Mamillius, Antigonus and the mariners, which cannot be redeemed by time. In Nicholas Hytner's 2001 National Theatre production, these elements were enhanced by a sense of awkwardness in the reunion of Leontes and Hermione, by the distinctly cool reaction of Paulina to Leontes's sudden proposal that she should marry Camillo, and by the concluding image of Hermione and Perdita, not having gone off with the others, 'clutching each other like shipwreck survivors' in the words of the reviewer Paul Taylor. Perhaps this is going too much against the grain of the text, but there is no doubting the ambiguities with which Shakespeare has invested the ending. Even Leontes's final line, 'Hastily lead away', raises questions. Why should Paulina lead off the assembled company, when normally the king would leave first? And why 'hastily', when he has just anticipated that a 'leisurely' recounting of their stories is in prospect? As always, Shakespeare leaves his theatrical interpreters with enormous scope for alternative stagings.

Many of the play's recurring images are rounded off in this scene. Paulina draws attention to the play's likeness to 'an old tale' which might be 'hooted at', yet hooting is the very last response that the scene evokes, suggesting that a 'winter's tale' may not necessarily be something trivial and laughable. The recurring processes of time and seasonal change are invoked again in Perdita's reference to the queen who 'ended when I but began', and Camillo's description of Leontes's sorrow, 'Which sixteen winters cannot blow away, | So many summers dry'. The 'statue' of Hermione arouses further consideration of the relationship between art and nature, representing both; and the art of the theatre, in particular, is suggested by the metatheatrical qualities of the whole scene, as staged by Paulina. Leontes himself is aware that, in the words of Jaques in *As You Like It*, 'all the world's a stage', when he ends the play by suggesting that each of them should 'answer to his part | Performed in this wide gap of time'. A feeling of intense satisfaction is engendered in the audience by their knowledge that they have already been privileged spectators of all the events that the characters must now share with each other in their offstage telling of their own tales.

Characters and characterisation

One of the most common errors made by students is to write about characters in literature as if they were real people. In reality, they are linguistic constructs created to fulfil a range of purposes in different texts. While an assessment of the 'personality' of a fictional or dramatic character may be a valid part of literary analysis, it is much more relevant to examine characterisation — the techniques a writer uses to create particular characters for particular purposes. When it comes to a play, the 'text' belonging to each character is a blueprint for interpretation by different actors, and one important aspect of analysis is to consider the range of potential performances that a text makes available.

Modern readers and audiences often look for psychological consistency in the portrayal of character, but this concept would have been alien to Shakespeare and his contemporaries. Characters function at each moment in a play script according to the dramatic needs of that moment, and while there may often be a clear sense of consistency or development, characters in Jacobean drama are equally often contradictory and ambiguous. An illusion of coherence can be created in performance by the fact that a single actor is playing the role, and the overall effect is often to suggest the inconsistency and complexity of real people.

Characters in a play are defined through language and action. What they do, what they say, how they say it, and what other characters say about them determine the response of a reader, while on stage these techniques of characterisation are enhanced by costume, gesture, facial expression and other performance features. In examining the text, you need to be sensitive to the characters' use of verse or prose, the rhetorical and figurative qualities of their speech, the imagery they use and that associated with them, and the tone of their language. Characters who are given soliloquies are placed in a privileged position in relation to members of the audience, who are allowed to share their innermost thoughts.

The notes that follow offer some general pointers to approaching the characters in *The Winter's Tale*; a more detailed response has already been offered in the scene summaries and commentary section (pages 30–62), which you should use in conjunction with this section.

Leontes

As a study in jealousy, Leontes stands alongside other Shakespearean husbands and lovers such as Claudio in *Much Ado about Nothing*, Othello, and Posthumus in *Cymbeline*. Leontes is unique, however, in that his jealousy is entirely self-generated, whereas the others are victims of Machiavellian hoaxers. Perhaps the nearest to Leontes is Ford in *The Merry Wives of Windsor*, though he at least has partial grounds for his jealous suspicions inasmuch as Falstaff is indeed pursuing his wife, despite her rejection of his advances.

For hundreds of years, Shakespeare's characterisation of Leontes was criticised because the onset of his jealousy appears so sudden and unmotivated. In an attempt to assert the character's psychological realism, some critics have argued that Leontes is already jealous before the play begins, and that his language indicates this. Others, such as the actor Antony Sher, who played the role in 1999, have sought explanations in the clinical diagnosis of certain psychoses that do indeed strike the victim without warning. These are modern preoccupations, however, and Shakespeare is concerned not with convincing psychological explanations but with the need to get the story off to a flying start, since he knows he does not have the leisure of the entire play's length to develop a fully-motivated portrayal of character. It is not the cause of Leontes's jealousy that he is concerned with, but its effects, on himself, his family and his kingdom.

Shakespeare creates Leontes's disturbed mental state through a number of linguistic features, notably his handling of the verse and his use of imagery. Though the rhythms of the iambic pentameter pound strongly beneath the surface of the verse, they are disrupted by a variety of factors. Irregularly placed stresses and lines longer or shorter than the standard ten syllables combine with the use of both enjambement and caesura to overlay the metre with the rhythms of ordinary speech. Grammatical structures are complex, often parenthetical and sometimes incomplete, creating a sense of both spontaneity and incoherence. Repetition of words and phrasing creates a sense of obsessive paranoia. Sound effects such as assonance, onomatopoeia and, particularly, alliteration, evoke the violence of a passion that is embodied in the very physicality of the language through which it is expressed. And the persistent imagery of sickness and infection suggests a man in the grip of a diseased imagination whose symptoms are evident in both his language and his behaviour.

All of this is a gift to an actor, if not to an editor. A passage such as that beginning 'Can thy dam? May't be? Affection [...]' (I.2.137–46) has been the cause of many an editorial headache, since it is not susceptible to any kind of coherent paraphrase. In the theatre, though, its sense is clear enough, and its incoherence stands as an apt signifier of Leontes's tortured mental state. Shakespeare's skilful use of the simple conjunction 'and', used six times, with increasingly deranged insistence, in the last five lines of the speech, carries the actor to a breathless climax that demands some physical manifestation to take over from language — hyperventilation, perhaps, or a fevered mopping of the brows that are 'hard'ning' into the cuckold's horns. Inevitably, the brief exchange between Hermione and Polixenes that follows — 'What means Sicilia?'; 'He something seems unsettled' (I.2.146–47) — has the impact of comic understatement or bathos, and this leads to a feature of Leontes's role that is often overlooked.

In many respects, Leontes is conceived as a comic character; his violent outbursts are simultaneously terrifying and ludicrous. There is scope for more obvious comedy in his statement that 'many a man there is, even at this present, | Now, while I speak this, holds his wife by th'arm, | That little thinks she has been sluiced in's absence, | [...] by his next neighbour' (I.2.192–95), if the actor delivers it directly to specific members of the audience. But it is principally when Paulina enters the action that Leontes is thrown into relief as a comic figure, no more able than Antigonus to control this forceful defender of common sense. He is potentially at his most comic when Paulina compares the baby's features with those of the father, and the way different productions have staged this, perhaps with the Lords cooing over the baby on one side and casting glances of comparison at the glowering Leontes on the other, frequently plays up its comic qualities.

Leontes's repentance, motivated by the news of Mamillius's death, is as sudden as the onset of his jealousy, and equally unconvincing to unsympathetic critics. Shakespeare is careful, though, to adjust his language gradually from the somewhat jerky breathlessness of his confession (III.2.150–69), with its long, complex sentence structures suggesting a need to unburden himself as rapidly as he can, to the more even pace of his formal conclusion to the scene, setting the tone for his sustained period of 'recreation' (III.2.237). Lacking the closure of a rhyming couplet, which Shakespeare avoids in this play as a marker of scene endings, his speech even ends on a half line, a subtle indication that his story is not yet complete.

The Leontes of Act V is a changed man linguistically as much as temperamentally. His verse is more regular, its rhythms calm and measured, and his vocabulary is now steeped in the imagery of grace and virtue. He is no less interesting a character, though, and there is something still suggestive of an obsessive personality in his complete dependence on Paulina. This is a man who has inflicted severe emotional damage on himself which even the passing of 16 years has not alleviated, and his role here is just as challenging for an actor as the more obvious histrionics of Acts I–III. It is a truism that goodness is harder to portray than evil, and it is a mark of the playwright's skill that he provides plenty of material for the actor to suggest both depth and complexity in the penitent Leontes, and to render him deserving of the miraculous reunions with which he is blessed.

(See also sample essay 3 (pages 128–30), which offers a comparison of one of Leontes's speeches from Act V with one from earlier in the play.)

Hermione

It is easy to generalise about Hermione's character through seeing her in terms of abstract qualities such as dignity, courage, graciousness, endurance and honour. To do so, however, is to diminish the touches of real humanity that Shakespeare invests her with, which are partly shown through the development of her character over the course of the four scenes in which she appears.

In Act I scene 2 it is her wit that predominates, taking the form of a light, bantering tone of affectionate mockery directed against both Polixenes and Leontes.

Her state of advanced pregnancy, easily forgotten when reading the play, is of course visually obvious on stage, adding to the sense of a mature woman quite at ease in her circle of family and friends. It would be a mistake to present her as a paragon, and there are occasions when her wit can seem tiresome, especially when she prevents the person she is speaking to from getting a word in, often by articulating a stream of questions without allowing space for an answer; this happens with Polixenes at I.2.46–56 and Leontes at I.2.90–101. When it becomes clear that something has upset Leontes, Hermione says nothing for around 25 lines, between her observation of his 'brow of much distraction' (I.2.149) and her apparently spontaneous announcement that she and Polixenes will adjourn to the garden.

An actor has many choices about what to do with Hermione's silence and how to motivate her departure with Polixenes. It is certainly possible for her to register a distinct awareness that all is not well, since on her next appearance, at the start of Act II scene 1, she is expressing irritation with Mamillius and has to allow her ladies to entertain him until she recovers herself. Though this could be attributed to the physical tiredness of advanced pregnancy, there are other possibilities, and it is notable that she chooses the 'merry' option for Mamillius's story (II.1.24), perhaps as a contrast to her own anxiety, only to be overruled by him. Essentially, though, this scene of touching domestic intimacy establishes a warm and close relationship between mother and son — a closeness that would have been unusual in many aristocratic households, in which the mother would have little contact with her young children.

Leontes's shocking disruption of this domestic harmony is greeted by Hermione with dignified disbelief expressed in tones of calm rebuke that nevertheless conceal a subtext of genuine anger, something emphasised by her triple repetition of the word 'villain' (II.1.78–80) even as she denies its application to Leontes, and her assertion that a subsequent apology from Leontes would 'scarce [...] right [her] throughly' (II.1.99–100). In denying herself the stereotypical female behaviour of 'weeping' (II.1.108), she paradoxically engages our pity even while assuming we will withhold it. Her patience, practicality and dignified testimony of her innocence arouse our admiration, and she is virtually granted the status of martyr in her belief that 'This action I now go on | Is for my better grace' (II.1.121–22). Her parting words to Leontes have a quiet and moving simplicity that nevertheless manages to deliver a stinging rebuke:

> Adieu, my lord.
> I never wished to see you sorry; now
> I trust I shall.   (II.1.122–24)

Recent productions of the play have often presented a shockingly altered Hermione in the trial scene, a physical wreck debilitated by long exposure to harsh prison conditions. This is at odds with the comparatively comfortable regime that would have been enjoyed by royal prisoners in Shakespeare's time, but it offers a salutary dramatic shock, and contrasts powerfully with the dignified demeanour she shows in her eloquent self-defence. In a series of speeches that build to a powerful emotional climax, she moves from a wryly realistic comment on her own credibility in the face of Leontes's predetermined opinion, to a moving account of her sufferings that avoids self-pity through a carefully controlled channelling of wronged innocence and righteous anger. From the moment of her arrest, she has put her faith in heavenly powers, and her defence reaches a climax in her appeal to the oracle: 'Apollo be my judge!' (III.2.114). It is entirely characteristic of Shakespeare that he follows this with her quite unexpected reference to her parentage: 'The Emperor of Russia was my father' (III.2.117), in a final assertion of her royal status. Her dignity can only be toppled, quite literally, by the ultimate blow of her son's death, coming only seconds after the oracle's declaration of her innocence.

It is as pointless to question either the motivation or the mechanics of Hermione's clandestine 16-year self-preservation as it is to speculate on the likelihood of her agreeing to impersonate a statue. In the play's own terms, these things are accepted as given. Much more important is to perceive Hermione's behaviour in the final scene, and to listen to her single speech. Fortunately, Shakespeare incorporates stage directions in the spoken text, from which it is possible to gather that she makes no gesture to Leontes until Paulina tells him to 'present [his] hand' to her (V.3.107), but that she then 'embraces him' (V.3.111). Critics have made much of the fact that she says nothing to Leontes, but these gestures clearly carry the weight of forgiveness, reconciliation and love. She uses her only speech to call down blessings on her daughter, identifying her as the sole motivation for her determined survival though she seems to have forgotten that she heard the oracle's pronouncements herself. Finally, there is clearly some business of a look exchanged, or perhaps avoided, with Polixenes, depending upon Leontes's ambiguous line, 'What! Look upon my brother' (V.3.147). However we interpret this, the Hermione of the play's conclusion is as different from her previous self as Leontes is from his. Reconciled and reunited they may be, but there remains a profound sense of loss and change as we think back to the vivacious and witty young wife and mother portrayed at the start of the play.

Polixenes

Polixenes is a straightforward character whose apparent changes in personality are determined purely by the needs of the plot. In Act I he is the injured innocent, in Act IV the authoritarian father and in Act V the wondering observer. Modern actors, however, often feel the need to deepen his individual traits and create for him a psychological journey that suggests a consistent line of development across the timescale of the play. Such a journey inevitably begins with his childhood friendship with Leontes. This idyllic relationship dominates the opening of the play and is prioritised in the dialogue above that of Leontes and Hermione, both in Camillo's extended celebration of it in the opening scene and in Polixenes's later account to Hermione. If their childhood innocence was a kind of Eden, it was an Eden corrupted not by the serpent but by Eve, in the person of their respective wives (see I.2.67–86).

Polixenes seems entirely at ease in Sicilia — hardly surprising after a nine-month visit —and his motivation to return home seems to be the desire to see his son again, something that Hermione recognises (I.2.34–37) and he himself implicitly admits in his account of his relationship with the prince, who he claims has a curative psychological power upon him (I.2.165–71). In admitting that he is subject to 'Thoughts that would thick [his] blood', Polixenes unknowingly links himself with Leontes, and it becomes ironic that, when it comes to the push, neither Florizel nor Mamillius can actually exert the curative power that both fathers claim for them. Already, the actor has deeper passions to tap into. When faced with Camillo's revelation of Leontes's jealousy, Polixenes's reaction is one of outraged innocence. The plot, though, requires him to take Camillo's advice and flee for his life, with only a passing thought for Hermione's situation: 'Good expedition be my friend and comfort | The gracious queen' (I.2.458–59). His actions might be subject to accusations of cowardice, and he admits, 'Fear o'ershades me' (I.2.457).

Sixteen years later, we find a bitter, unhappy Polixenes, presiding over a court partly sustained by a network of spies, faced with the disturbing behaviour of his son and the threatened loss of his chief adviser. When he talks of 'that fatal country Sicilia' with its supposedly penitent king (IV.2.16–18), his bitterness can perhaps partly be ascribed to guilt at his role in the 'loss of his most precious queen and children' (IV.2.19). An actor will probably want to carry this guilt forward to Act V, to explain why Polixenes inaccurately identifies himself as 'him that was the cause of this' (V.3.54).

Polixenes is an unattractive character in Act IV. Although his concerns about Florizel would be entirely comprehensible to a Jacobean audience, the fact that Shakespeare presents the prince's relationship with Perdita as a romantic and attractive liaison, and that we know she is really a princess, and that, instead of confronting his son directly, Polixenes resorts to disguise, all render his behaviour singularly unsympathetic. He is hypocritical in his advocacy of the botanical grafting of 'A gentler scion to the wildest stock' (IV.4.93), in view of his unwillingness to countenance the same in social-class terms, and the cruelty of his threats to Perdita and her family when he reveals himself is out of all proportion to the offences they have committed. However, merely reading the text conceals an element that is evident in the theatre, namely the potentially comic impact of his and Camillo's disguises. Most productions choose to make them visually ludicrous, with unconvincing false beards or glasses, and it can be very funny if they have dressed in what they consider, quite mistakenly, to be appropriate clothing for a visit to the country.

With this dimension always in view, the force of Polixenes's anger is undermined and, as with the comic dimensions of Leontes's role, we are persistently reminded that the play is moving towards the resolution of comedy, not tragedy.

Polixenes cannot be excluded from the final scene, though there is little for him to do except to express amazement at the statue and its coming to life. A good actor, however, will convey a range of emotions in the scene, appearing at times both guilty and ill-at-ease, notably at that mysterious line of Leontes, 'What! Look upon my brother' (V.3.147). He must also convey Polixenes's pride and pleasure in the union of his son and Leontes's daughter, while joining the other characters in creating a sense of sadness and loss.

Camillo

In his role as trusted counsellor, first to Leontes and then to Polixenes, Camillo is a character type represented in Shakespeare's other last plays by Helicanus in *Pericles* and Gonzalo in *The Tempest*. All are characters of unswerving loyalty and integrity, but in Camillo's case these qualities are sorely tested. He begins in a choric role, as the source of crucial information about the childhood friendship of the two kings which he imparts to the audience via Archidamus. Soon, though, he is faced with a moral dilemma that puts his own life at risk. At first, he stands up for himself with spirit, defends Hermione's honesty, and rebukes Leontes with courage: 'You never spoke what did become you less | Than this' (I.2.282–83). But at the suggestion of poisoning Polixenes he is forced to prevaricate. He confesses that he has the skills for the job (I.2.318–21) and, since he 'must believe' the king (I.2.333), he agrees to take it on, providing Leontes takes no action against Hermione. His political astuteness is evident in his recognition of the importance of avoiding a damaging international scandal through 'The injury of tongues in courts and kingdoms | Known and allied to yours' (I.2.338–39).

In soliloquy (I.2.351–64), Camillo reveals his true feelings. His obedience to Leontes is outweighed by his moral probity, leaving him no option but to 'Forsake the court'. At first reluctant to tell Polixenes the reason for Leontes's altered behaviour, he is forced by his sense of honour to do so, counselling flight. Perhaps, though, there is an element of moral cowardice in all this, as Camillo plans to use his considerable political authority to ensure the secret evacuation of Sicilia by the entire Bohemian delegation, claiming not only that it is 'safer to | Avoid what's grown than question how 'tis born', but prioritising his fears for his own safety when he tells Polixenes that if he 'seek to prove' the truth of what he has told him, 'I dare not stand by' (I.2.443–44). What is noticeably absent from their discussion is any consideration of what might happen to Hermione, and as the play develops, Camillo's self-preservation is thrown into relief by the notable courage of Paulina in standing up to Leontes on behalf of justice, with complete disdain for any punishment he may inflict on her.

When Camillo next appears, it is as Polixenes's trusted and indispensable adviser, whose management of the king's affairs cannot possibly be handed over to anyone else (IV.2.11–13). Polixenes is therefore reluctant to grant Camillo's request to return to Sicilia, which Camillo apparently accepts with a good grace, entering freely into the discussion of Prince Florizel's activities.

At the sheep-shearing, Camillo is obviously impressed with Perdita's beauty (see IV.4.109–10, 160–61), but says very little during the festivities until after Polixenes's angry departure. One would expect him to go off with the king, but his remaining behind indicates that he has his own purposes to pursue, which soon become apparent. In helping Florizel and Perdita, there is no doubt that he gives them sound advice, though one might question the political wisdom of his condoning a match between the heir to the throne and a shepherdess. However, his motives are essentially selfish, since circumstances offer him the possibility of the return to Sicilia that he craves.

There is something almost machiavellian about his plans, expressed in the terminology of self-interest: 'Now were I happy if | His going I could frame to serve my turn' (IV.4.487–88). Interestingly, his phrasing echoes that of Iago, one of Shakespeare's most devious schemers, who says of Othello, 'I follow him to serve my turn upon him' (*Othello*, I.1.42). Camillo's planning is swift and sure-footed, its practical details flowing from him in fluent and confident verse; one can see here what has made him, for Polixenes, the consummate management executive. He is as adept at seizing passing opportunities, such as his exploitation of Autolycus's potential for a clothes swap with Florizel, as at devising complicated action plans with purposeful spontaneity. Though we know his motives are partly selfish, it is still something of a shock, towards the end of the scene, when he confides to the audience, 'What I do next shall be to tell the king | Of this escape and whither they are bound' (IV.4.631–32). Even if his plans go awry for Florizel and Perdita, Camillo will at least succeed in fulfilling his own desire to 're-view Sicilia' (IV.4.635).

We do not see Camillo at all as his plan takes its course; by the final scene its success has been assured beyond his wildest dreams. In his two short speeches here, he gently rebukes Leontes for the excessive duration of his sorrow and, when Hermione's statue comes to life, requests that she should speak. Though he himself says no more, his story is not quite over. In an unexpected twist that generally elicits laughter in performance, Leontes pairs him off with the widowed Paulina, hinting that he has privately expressed an interest in marrying her: 'For him, I partly know his mind' (V.3.142).

It is difficult to question Leontes's final assessment of Camillo's 'worth and honesty' which can be 'justified | By [...] a pair of kings' (V.3.144–46), but a good actor in the role will also have shown during the play a character driven partly by self-preservation and self-interest; one who motivated Hartley Coleridge in 1851 to comment, 'Camillo is an old rogue whom I can hardly forgive for his double treachery'.

Antigonus

Like Camillo, Antigonus is faced with a painful moral dilemma in which his sworn loyalty to the king comes into conflict with the demands of simple human decency. Introduced in Act II scene 1, he remains silent until after Hermione has been removed to prison, at which point his disbelief and indignation take fire, supported by the other lords. Utterly convinced of Hermione's innocence, he assumes that Leontes is the victim of 'some putter-on' or 'villain' (II.1.141,142) — but in this play, unlike *Othello* or *Cymbeline*, no such character is required to instigate the protagonist's jealousy. Convinced that if Hermione is an adulteress then no woman is to be trusted, Antigonus says he will chain his wife to him and 'geld' his three daughters (II.1.143–50) if she is proved to be unfaithful. Though his threat is merely a rhetorical device to emphasise his conviction, it does demonstrate the power of male authority. In retrospect, we might view Antigonus's forceful speeches in an ironic light: his wife, Paulina, proves to be the dominant partner in their marriage, unlikely to submit to any such treatment of herself or their children; and, painfully, Antigonus meets his death believing in the very thing he has denied with such passion — Hermione's guilt. Though he recognises that Leontes's behaviour will ultimately arouse only 'laughter' (II.1.198), he does not survive to enjoy the truth of his prediction.

In Act II scene 3 it only gradually becomes clear that Paulina, who was introduced in the previous scene, is Antigonus's wife. Shakespeare uses their relationship to lighten the tone with the conventional comedy of a shrewish wife and her hen-pecked husband, though both of them retain their dignity despite the familiar stereotyping. On Paulina's departure, however, events take a serious turn for Antigonus, who is trapped by his own compassion into a solemn oath to perform whatever Leontes commands in order to save the baby's life. Modern audiences are likely to be critical of Antigonus's actions in exposing the child to its fate; after all, he could have ensured its safety and Leontes would have been none the wiser. This, though, is to ignore the powerful code of honour that operated in Renaissance culture, and the moment where Antigonus is made to swear obedience on the king's sword needs to be staged with an impressive simplicity that matches the impact of the language:

LEONTES   [...] Swear by this sword
　　　　Thou wilt perform my bidding.
ANTIGONUS   I will, my lord.
LEONTES Mark, and perform it — see'st thou? [...]
　　　　　　　　　　　　　　　　(II.3.167–69)

By Antigonus's moral standards, he now has no choice, though his pity for the child is palpable in his parting speech, as is his implied condemnation of Leontes's cruelty (II.3.183–91).

Antigonus's role in the play ends in an impressive, if rather strange, soliloquy and an ignominious exit — the most notorious departure from the stage in Shakespeare. His interpretation of Hermione's appearance to him in a dream is flawed, and one of the play's passing tragedies is that he dies believing her guilty of adultery. Shakespeare makes it clear why he goes through with his task, as he observes, 'most accursed am I | To be by oath enjoined to this' (III.3.51–52). Whether his pursuit by the bear should be terrifyingly dramatic or ludicrously comic is a matter that has long been debated; what is certain is that the Clown's subsequent account of his death translates it into pitiful comedy. The play does not forget him, though. Paulina evidently feels his loss deeply even after 16 years (see V.1.40–44, V.2.57–60), and the 3rd Gentleman speculates that his death represented divine punishment for his role in exposing the child (V.2.56–57). His death, along with that of Mamillius, haunts the play's positive resolution.

Paulina

Entirely Shakespeare's invention, Paulina is a pivotal figure in the scheme of the play. Though partly conceived as the sharp-tongued shrewish wife, or scold, she transcends the stereotypical features of such roles to become a powerful advocate for truth and justice. Her authority is evident on her very first appearance, as she orders her attendants to summon the Gaoler, whom she assumes will jump to attention on hearing her name: 'Let him have knowledge who I am' (II.2.2). She is forthright, outspoken and determined, not afraid to speak openly of the king's 'dangerous, unsafe lunes' (II.2.30) and confident of her own power over him:

> He must be told on't, and he shall. The office
> Becomes a woman best; I'll take't upon me.   (II.2.31–32)

Shakespeare is careful to make it clear how Paulina is regarded in the court: the Gaoler knows her for 'a worthy lady, | And one who much I honour' (II.2.5–6), while Emilia also calls her 'worthy', praises her 'honour' and 'goodness', and asserts that 'There is no lady living | So meet for this great errand' (II.2.42–46). The errand itself, however, shows a somewhat unrealistic side to Paulina's self-confidence: when she says, 'We do not know | How he may soften at the sight o'th'child' (II.2.39–40), we are sceptical of her assessment, though Hermione herself has evidently had the same idea (II.2.47–49).

Paulina's behaviour in the remainder of Acts I–III builds on the expectations aroused in this introductory scene, showing her moral and physical courage in action as she dominates the court in her two powerful confrontations with Leontes. In Act II scene 3 she bursts into his presence despite the lords' protestations, professing to be the 'physician' (II.3.54) who will 'bring him sleep' (II.3.33), courageously resisting all attempts to remove her from the chamber by force (II.3.61–64, 124–26), and contemptuously rebuffing his threats to have her burnt: 'I care not: | It is an heretic that makes the fire, | Not she which burns in't' (II.3.113–14). She also brings comedy into the play, at Leontes's expense, beginning with his rueful rebuke to Antigonus, 'I charged thee that she should not come about me. | I knew she would' (II.3.43–44). Shakespeare gives vocal strength to her outbursts through technical devices such as alliteration and assonance, helping the actor to articulate the force of her anger. A passage such as her speech at lines 82–89, for example, repays attention for its emphatic reiteration of the initial consonants b, s, c and r, and its repeated long vowel sounds in the phrases 'Babe's, betrays', 'remove | The root', 'oak or stone'.

In our admiration for her fiery indignation, though, it is easy to overlook her culpability in leaving the baby unprotected in the presence of a patently demented tyrant, whom she herself has effectively called so (II.3.115–19), and a collection of impotent courtiers. We do not see her response to the child's removal, by her own husband, to its exposure and almost inevitable death, but it is notable that, though her presence is demanded in the trial scene, she remains silent until Hermione faints on the news of Mamillius's death (III.2.145–46). It is up to the actor to determine whether Paulina's demeanour during the proceedings should indicate any sense of remorse at her part in what has happened.

Paulina comes into her own again, however, in her announcement of the queen's death, which she delays with rhetorical skill for the space of 27 lines, during which she takes the opportunity to give Leontes a powerful resumé of his stupidity and wickedness, accompanied by sarcasm and insult. An actor must play this, I think, as if Hermione were indeed dead, and not try to indicate Paulina's awareness that she is delivering a lie; no doubt must be awakened in either her fictional or real audience that she is playing a dangerous game of bluff when she asserts 'I say she's dead; I'll swear't', and offers to take Leontes to view her body (III.2.200–01). In retrospect, there is an irony in her exhortation of Leontes not to 'repent these things' (III.2.205), since the gods will never grant him forgiveness even if he spends 10,000 years in painful penance; in the event, it only takes 16 years for him to be redeemed, at least in human terms.

Though Leontes accepts her justifiable righteous anger, his lords are shocked at her departure from decorum, declaring that she has 'made fault | I'th'boldness of [her] speech' (III.2.214–15). She accepts their rebuke, defending herself by retreating behind the stereotype of female 'rashness' (III.2.218) and calling herself 'a foolish woman' (III.2.224). Her manipulation of his feelings continues more subtly, however, in reminding him of his queen, his children and even her own lost husband in the very act of saying she will not do so — a rhetorical technique known as *occupatio* (III.2.225–28). Her rhetoric ends in the promise to 'say nothing' (III.2.229).

Sixteen years later it appears as if Paulina's role in Leontes's court has become that of guardian of Hermione's memory. Time may have mellowed her, but she is still adept at using her linguistic skill to prick Leontes's conscience, painfully referring to Hermione as 'she you killed' (V.1.15), and continuing to draw rebukes from the courtiers for her lack of tact and diplomacy (V.1.20–23). There is a sense of urgency to her constant reminders of Hermione's qualities, since there is political pressure on the king to remarry, and her evocation of the late queen's vengeful ghost, 'shriek[ing]' in passionate bitterness at any new wife (V.1.56–67), has the same grotesque quality as Antigonus's vision of Hermione in Act III scene 3. Only now does Shakespeare begin to hint, through Paulina, that Hermione is not dead; making Leontes swear 'never to marry but by [her] free leave' (V.1.70), she imagines a new queen 'not [...] so young | As was your former', who will only exist 'when your first queen's again in breath' (V.1.78–83).

The arrival of Florizel and Perdita shifts the focus from Paulina, but Shakespeare twice derives amusement from her jealousy, on Hermione's behalf, of Perdita's beauty, first rebuking the servant who praises her (V.1.93–112) and later the apparently love–struck Leontes (V.1.222–26). She is a central figure in the conversation of the gentlemen in Act V scene 2, not just in the account of her 'noble combat [...] 'twixt joy and sorrow', with 'one eye declined for the loss of her husband, another elevated that the oracle was fulfilled' (V.2.58–60), but in the mysterious account of her regular visits to the 'removed house' (V.2.85) where Julio Romano's statue of Hermione has been 'many years in doing and now newly performed' (V.2.76–77).

Paulina is a consummate master of ceremonies in the final scene, yet paradoxically she seems humbler and more restrained than anywhere else in the play, thanking Leontes and Polixenes for visiting her 'poor house' (V.3.6) and offering a moving apology for all her former behaviour: 'What [...] | I did not well, I meant well' (V.3.2–3). She manages the gradual build-up of suspense with subtlety and skill, tempting her audience to demand more even while threatening to end the performance, three times attempting to close the curtain that has revealed the statue (V.3.59, 68, 83). As she moves to the climax of her show, she is eager to deny the involvement of 'wicked powers' and disclaims that she is engaged in 'unlawful business' (V.3.91, 96) — a reminder, perhaps, that Leontes once referred to her as a 'mankind witch' (II.3.67). When Hermione finally moves, it is under direct instruction from Paulina, who is required to speak stage directions to all the characters at this point, such is their wonder: she tells Leontes to present his hand to his wife (V.3.107), Perdita to kneel to her mother (V.3.119–20) and Hermione to turn to her daughter (V.3.120). Paulina ends her spoken role with wry self-pity, contrasting herself with the 'precious winners all' (V.3.131) and lamenting her own old age and widowhood (V.3.132–35). When she is unexpectedly offered the hand of Camillo, Shakespeare gives her no response, leaving an actor to determine how she feels; but her key role in the play is recognised by Leontes who, against the normal conventions of precedence in a dramatic exit, invites her to 'Hastily lead away' the assembled company (V.3.155).

The Shepherd

The Shepherd fulfils many roles in the play, marked by appropriate shifts in the style, form and tone of his language. Partly a conventional pastoral figure and partly a realistic portrayal of a well-to-do countryman, he also veers between the dignified host of the sheep-shearing festivities, proud of his family and his status, and the comic butt of Autolycus's trickery. The greatest contrast within his character occurs during Act IV scene 4. In the first part of the scene, Shakespeare matches his status with that of the other characters by giving him lively and varied blank verse speeches, two of which in particular demonstrate the lack of condescension with which he is portrayed. First, there is his affectionate evocation of his late wife and her bustling activity on previous festive occasions, recalled in order to urge Perdita to emulate her outgoing personality (IV.4.55-70). There is something dignified and moving in his pride, and in the speech's focus on the spiritual productivity of friendship and hospitality. In contrast, his despairing speech after the unmasking of Polixenes and Florizel (IV.4.430–41) is an impressive outburst of justified anger. Although its tone is full of self-pity, the verse, the simple vocabulary and the homely imagery elevate it to a level of moving dignity that elicits our genuine sympathy.

When he returns at the end of the scene, however, it is as if we are seeing a different character. His verse has become prose, his linguistic skill has become comic ignorance, and his generous hospitality has become self-interest, his only concern being to save his own skin by revealing the truth of Perdita's origins. Though in Act V he and his son turn the tables on Autolycus, they are still presented as comically ignorant rustics, amusingly revelling in their new gentlemanly status. Consistency of characterisation is not Shakespeare's concern here, and we simply have to accept the Shepherd at face value as he appears in each successive scene. To restore his dignity, as some productions do, by granting him and his son a place in the statue scene is probably a very modern notion, and one that would undoubtedly have been alien to Jacobean ideas of both dramatic and social decorum.

(See also sample essay 2 (pages 127–28), which gives a full analysis of the Shepherd's first speech in Act III scene 3.)

The Clown

Among the various stock character types of Elizabethan drama, it is important to distinguish between the comic functions of the Fool and the Clown. The Fool is the licensed court jester, whose often satirical wit usually makes him one of the most intelligent characters in a play. Touchstone in *As You Like It*, Feste in *Twelfth Night* and the Fool in *King Lear* are Shakespeare's most fully developed Fools. In complete contrast, the Clown is a rustic character whose uneducated simplicity is exploited for comic effect. Such characters appear in both large and small roles in plays such as *Titus Andronicus*, *Love's Labour's Lost*, *Othello* and *Antony and Cleopatra*. Though these character types are almost complete opposites, Shakespeare

sometimes combines their qualities in characters who are both clownish and witty, such as Lancelot Gobbo in *The Merchant of Venice*.

To modern sensibilities the designation of an uneducated countryman as 'clown' seems patronising and demeaning, and some recent productions of *The Winter's Tale* have tried to avoid such condescension by designating Perdita's foster-brother as 'Young Shepherd' or 'Shepherd's Son'. Perhaps this is unnecessary, since in creating him, Shakespeare has both exploited and transcended the stereotypical qualities of the conventional Clown. We may be invited to laugh at his simplicity, naïvety and gullibility, and at his linguistic and arithmetical inadequacies, but we might also admire many of his qualities. He shows compassion in burying Antigonus's remains, and in helping Autolycus, whom he takes to be the victim of a violent robbery. He deals with his rival lovers, Mopsa and Dorcas, with sensitivity, eventually promising, 'wenches, I'll buy for you both' (IV.4.294). His unaffected enthusiasm for ballads is infectious, and in performance he is often shown to be one of the liveliest and jolliest participants in the dancing. He is an immensely likeable character, despite the fact that it is he who urges his father to disclaim Perdita as his daughter (IV.4.652–61). We enjoy seeing him gain the upper hand over Autolycus at the end, and respond warmly to his relish of his enhanced social status, expressed in entertaining linguistic contortions. It is the Clown rather than Autolycus who brings a sympathetic warmth to the play's comedy.

Autolycus

Autolycus erupts into the play with invigorating energy; after the solemnity of the preceding events, the last thing we expect is a singing con-man, particularly when we have just been led to anticipate an introduction to Florizel and Perdita. His cheerful amorality acts as a corrective to events in Sicilia; compared with the psychotic cruelty of Leontes, his criminality is trivial and even admirable, particularly as no one genuinely suffers as a result of his activities. What we admire are his light-heartedness, his performance skills, his wit and his resilience, and we are grateful for his introduction of unrestrained physical and verbal comedy into the play. Shakespeare offers us enough details about his life and background to give him an air of reality — his former service of Florizel (IV.3.13–14), his inheriting of his trade from his father (IV.3.23–25), his evocation of the all-too-real dangers of his way of life (IV.3.27–28) and his local reputation (IV.3.87–88); essentially, though, we take him at face value.

Autolycus only has two big opportunities to work the audience: in his fleecing of the Clown and his incarnation as the ballad-monger. After this, his singing is silenced and he himself becomes largely an instrument of the plot. Dramatically, his role goes into decline, and he is only restored to something of his old self in his mockery of the Shepherd and Clown at the end of Act IV scene 4. However, since their world has now crumbled about their ears, Autolycus's trickery no longer has quite the same sense of fun. By Act V he is reduced to being the silent recipient of the Gentlemen's narrative revelations, before being bested by his erstwhile victims. It is a surprising dramatic falling-off, marked by his ignominious verbal submission in promising to 'amend [his] life' (V.2.124) and 'prove' a 'tall fellow of [his] hands' (V.2.136–38). For an actor, this must be frustrating; for the play, it is vital: a lively musical climax for Autolycus would detract from the solemn impact of the concluding scene.

Perdita

Like Miranda in *The Tempest*, Perdita can appear somewhat insipid. Unlike the heroines of Shakespeare's other last plays, Marina in *Pericles* and Imogen in *Cymbeline*, she is not faced with physical and moral hazards that she has to confront for herself, since she always has Florizel beside her. Her modesty (IV.4.9), her unease at the 'borrowed flaunts' (IV.4.23) of her role as festive hostess, her anxiety about the outcome of her relationship with the prince (IV.4.35–40), her shyness (IV.4.67), her condemnation of botanical interbreeding (IV.4.86–88), her romantic flower poetry (IV.4.116–29) and her prim concern about the possible scurrility of the pedlar's songs (IV.4.207) are all calculated to diminish her appeal to a modern audience. In Shakespeare's time, however, they would probably have been regarded as glowing testimonials to her feminine virtues.

There is little material in her role to make her into a more feisty heroine, but plenty to reduce her status as a model of virtue. She is, after all, engaged in a serious deception with unpredictable domestic and political consequences, and her courage when the inevitable crisis occurs (IV.4.421–25) is marked by a singular failure to address any explanation to her father; no wonder he calls her 'cursèd wretch' (IV.4.437) before he leaves in despair. To Florizel she can only say the equivalent of 'I told you so' (IV.4.453), and her brave words about moral courage (IV.4.555–56) are spoken in a virtual vacuum, being two of the merely ten or so lines that she speaks in the space of the 200 during which Florizel and Camillo organise a course of action. She herself partly explains this, in denying her own articulacy (IV.4.359–60). In Act V she speaks only three times: once, at last, to express sympathy for the Shepherd — while also bewailing her own misfortune (V.1.201–03); once to kneel and beg the blessing of Hermione's statue (V.3.42–46); and once to echo Leontes's willingness to gaze at it for 20 years (V.3.84–85). The climax of her role, her response to her mother's reanimation, is silent but steeped in emotion.

What all this reveals, in part, is the different expectations that we may have of a dramatic character from those prevalent in Shakespeare's time. Perdita is essentially character as symbol, and her function in the play does not require us to respond to her as a complex or even sympathetic human being: it is what she represents, rather than her personality, that is important. She is the lost child found, the agent of reconciliation, the restorer of marital and political harmony. But this does not help

a modern actor, who must fill in all those blanks in her role, those long, passive silences, with a great deal of intent listening and visual response, though perhaps not much in the way of physical action.

Florizel

Florizel is a flawed hero, but again we must be careful of judging his role by modern standards of characterisation. Romantic, passionate, courageous and resourceful, his optimistic imagery works alongside that of Autolycus, whose opening song declared that 'the red blood reigns in the winter's pale' (IV.3.4), to evoke a mood of joyful celebration. 'Apprehend | Nothing but jollity,' declares Florizel (IV.4.24–25), and urges Perdita, 'let's be red with mirth' (IV.4.54). Yet Florizel might also be seen as being complacent, impulsive, rash, pompous and arrogant — the last two qualities demonstrated particularly in the tone of patronising superiority he takes in conversation with the disguised Polixenes:

> I yield all this;
> But for some other reasons, my grave sir,
> Which 'tis not fit you know, I not acquaint
> My father of this business. (IV.4.389–92)

Like Perdita, he demonstrates no sympathy for the Shepherd's distress; indeed, he immediately follows the old man's exit with the guiltily defensive, 'Why look you so upon me?' (IV.4.441), before affirming his determination not to cave in to his father's anger. Already well practised in deception, he carries off his arrival in Leontes's court in the role of Bohemian ambassador with persuasive diplomatic skill. These features of his character all serve to humanise him, so that we do not see him as an idealised fairy-tale figure, but it is important for the overall scheme of the play that he comes across essentially as a worthy match for Perdita, whose faults can be put down to his youth and to the admirable constancy of his love, which is not bound by the artificial dictates of social class barriers.

At all his key moments Florizel gains our approval. His optimism is infectious; his promise of chastity (IV.4.33–35) demonstrates his respect for Perdita; his praise of her qualities is expressed in some of the play's loveliest poetry (IV.4.135–46); his participation in the feasting and dancing shows his social skills to be free of all condescension; and his various expressions of love and constancy are forceful and impressive (e.g. IV.4.466–71, V.1.214–17). Some of the verse Shakespeare gives him is so powerful in its imagery that it would not be out of place on the lips of one of his tragic heroes, notably when he asserts that if he violates his faith, 'then | Let nature crush the sides o'th'earth together | And mar the seeds within!' (IV.4.456–58). He shows enormous warmth in his dealings with Camillo, and his willingness to take the advice of his father's trusted counsellor demonstrates humility and gratitude. He can even make a joke of their situation: 'Should I now meet my father, | He would not call me son' (IV.4.626–27). His dignity when he believes Camillo has betrayed him and he is forced to ask for Leontes's help and support is notable (V.1.217–21), and his courage and faithful love never waver. Shakespeare gives him no words during the final scene of the play, but his presence needs to be strongly felt in his physical relationship with Perdita, maintaining the love and support he has shown throughout as she deals with the emotional impact of her mother's restoration.

Minor characters

The secondary characters of *The Winter's Tale* are vividly realised, creating a three-dimensional social context for both the Sicilian court and the Bohemian country-side, animated, one assumes, by the same group of supporting actors. One reason why Polixenes's court, seen only in Act IV scene 2, is so empty, must be that all available actors are getting ready for the sheep-shearing scene.

Among the courtly characters, **Archidamus** is used partly to share information with the audience at the start of the play, and partly to suggest, through the artificiality of his prose style, something of the pretentious superficiality of court life. The three **Gentlemen** of Act V scene 2 are similarly used, as bearers of narrative information and indicators of courtly style. In both cases, the polite courtly façade is soon thrown into relief by the emotional rawness of the scenes that follow.

Leontes's lords and Hermione's ladies demonstrate another facet of court life. The **Lords** are loyal to Leontes but not uncritical of his behaviour, making constant attempts to defend Hermione, to stand up for Antigonus and to assert their influence. They prove impotent, however, and perhaps deserve Paulina's repeated rebukes (see II.3.33–36, 127–28), though even after her angry exit they kneel to beg the king to show mercy to the baby (II.3.148–52). **Cleomenes** and **Dion** hold a special position in the court; chosen as ambassadors to Apollo's oracle, they introduce a mood of transcendent religious serenity into the infected atmosphere of the play in Act III scene 1, and by Act V they have evidently been promoted to the status of senior advisers. Here, their role is to urge Leontes to consider remarriage for the sake of ensuring political stability through the production of an heir, leading to dramatic conflict with Paulina. The **Ladies** provide a tight circle of domesticity around Hermione. Their concerns are the traditionally feminine ones of child-bearing and childcare, and they discuss the queen's pregnancy in an attractively natural and colloquial manner (II.1.15–20). They are allowed to accompany Hermione to prison, and in Act II scene 2 **Emilia** emerges as her principal confidante — most productions sensibly make her one of the ladies we have already seen. She gives an account of Perdita's premature birth, and shows confident support of Paulina's 'goodness', which she interestingly describes using the imagery of childbirth: 'your free undertaking cannot miss | A thriving issue' (II.2.43–45).

Ironically, Leontes's existing issue, **Mamillius**, is very far from thriving, as the accusations against his mother have sent him into a physical decline from which he never recovers. We never see him in this state, though the 1999 RSC production presented him as a sickly child from the start, confined to a wheelchair and played by the actress who later played Perdita. Mamillius is a typical Shakespearean child's role, though his bantering wit is restricted when he is with his father, only emerging fully in the precocious prattle of his scene with the ladies. His winter's tale of 'sprites and goblins' (II.1.26) remains incomplete, though he continues it silently as attention shifts to his father. His death is one of the tragedies of the play that time cannot revoke, though Paulina keeps his memory alive (see V.1.115–18).

Occupying less elevated positions in Sicilia are the **Gaoler** and the **Mariner**, both of whom are sketched in by Shakespeare with effective touches of moral distaste for the tasks they are required to fulfil. The Gaoler's pity for Hermione is implicit in his respectful compliance with Paulina's requests, despite his anxiety about breaking the rules; while the Mariner is more openly critical, blaming the storm on divine anger (III.3.4–6) and expressing relief at the conclusion of such a detestable task (III.3.13–14). He also, in passing, prepares us for the possibility of 'creatures | Of prey' on the prowl (III.3.11–12).

Finally, there are various **Servants**, whose roles are principally functional, as providers of information — 'He took good rest tonight' (II.3.10); 'he hath not slept tonight' (II.3.31) — and bringers of news — 'The prince your son […] is gone' (III.2.141–42). Like the **Officer** who presides over the opening of the oracle, the actors of the servants have little scope for creating character, though there are exceptions, notably the servant who announces Florizel's arrival in Sicilia and is overcome with the beauty of his princess (V.1.85–112).

The subsidiary Bohemian characters are less individualised than those of the Sicilian court, their function being principally to evoke the celebratory mood through their communal involvement in the dancing and the enjoyment of Autolycus's performance as pedlar. The **Shepherds** and **Shepherdesses** who are guests at the festivities need to be distinguished from the **Herdsmen** who visit solely to perform their satyr-dance. None of these have individual spoken lines, functioning solely as purveyors of setting and atmosphere. **Mopsa** and **Dorcas**, however, are attractive roles for performers with a gift for character comedy. As rivals for the affections of the Clown, who currently favours Mopsa, they trade suggestive insults, demonstrate a craving for cheap trinkets, react with gullible amazement to Autolycus's far-fetched ballads and cheerfully join him in singing one that reflects their own amorous rivalry. Their mutual jealousy is a far cry from the destructive passion of Leontes. The **Shepherd's Servant** is almost as lively a role, in his enthusiastic introduction to the unexpected entertainers who turn up at the feast, first the pedlar (IV.4.181–205) and then the dancers (IV.4.306–21). To double this role with the servant-poet who introduces Perdita's arrival in

Sicilia with equally vigorous enthusiasm would provide a very satisfying cameo for an actor.

One character remains: **Time**. His rhyming couplets and narrative function demand a skilful and authoritative actor. His status as an allegorical abstraction does not prevent him from being characterised with human touches which it is up to the actor to devise. In particular, his lines create a direct relationship with the audience that can be effectively exploited (IV.1.15–17, 19–20, 29–32), his false modesty perhaps lending a humorous tone to his speech.

Language and style

Some linguistic difficulties

Language is not a fixed entity with a stable and immutable system of signification and usage. New words are created, old ones become redundant, while others change their meaning. Four hundred years is a long time in the life of a language, so it is hardly surprising that we find considerable differences between the language of a Shakespeare play and that of today. The 'rules' of modern English spelling, punctuation, grammar and syntax were not really established until the eighteenth century, and in Shakespeare's time language was much more flexible — we even find him inventing new words, or using existing ones in a context in which no one had used them before. Frequently we find evidence of a language in flux, with archaic and modern usages working side by side.

The impact of such changes on our understanding of Shakespeare's language is often exaggerated, however, and our difficulties with it are sometimes self-fulfilling — we expect it to be difficult, so we find it so. When we listen to the plays spoken by skilful actors, we understand parts that seemed obscure on the page. We may not grasp the meaning of every word, with all its subtleties of nuance and implication, but we follow the story, understand the characters and their relationships, and appreciate the ideas behind the play. The RSC's 2003 programmes made an important point: 'it is up to us, his audience, not to sit on each line with a dictionary but to become caught up in the live experience of theatre'.

Sometimes, the difficulties in Shakespeare do not reside in the language at all, but in the wealth of classical allusions or historical references that lie outside the frame of our own limited general knowledge. Or perhaps we are confronted by alien value systems or unfamiliar social structures that challenge our understanding. Linguistically, however, it can often be the richness of Shakespeare's metaphorical language that creates a barrier to our immediate understanding. We can be overwhelmed by figurative images at one remove from what is being described or the feelings that are being expressed — images which often tumble one over another in

a seemingly unstoppable flow. However, Shakespeare's language is poetry, and we should accept it as such. In responding to poetry, we are required to open our own imaginations to the mysterious power of words to make us see things afresh, from an unlikely angle or a startling perspective. 'Understanding' does not have to be limited to working out a literal meaning; it can be intuitive, imaginative or emotional. The language of poetry enriches us.

One striking feature of Jacobean usage is more important than it may at first seem. The second person pronoun varies between *you* and *thou*, with their associated possessive variants *your/thy* and *yours/thine*. There is, however, a rationale behind such variations which allows for a subtlety of implication not possible in modern English. *You* is always used in the plural, for example when Cleomenes and Dion are being put on oath in the trial scene:

> You here shall swear upon this sword of justice
> That, you, Cleomenes and Dion [...]   (III.2.122–23)

You could also be used to indicate respect, while *thou* could be used to suggest affection. Florizel and Perdita use both forms when speaking to each other. However, *thou* was also used to address social inferiors, and when used in an inappropriate social context could be regarded as an insult. These shadings of implication are often lost on modern readers and audiences, but can help actors to assess the tone of the discourse in which they are engaged.

Verse and prose

Verse is language that is organised rhythmically according to particular patterns of metre and the arrangement of lines. In plays of Shakespeare's time and earlier, verse was the conventional medium of dramatic discourse. Plays were not regarded as naturalistic slices of life, and the heightened language of verse was felt to be appropriate to their non-realistic status as performance texts. However, dramatists increasingly varied the range of their dramatic language to include speeches and scenes in prose, the language of everyday speech and writing. Verse tended to be given to noble and royal characters, expressing romantic or elevated feelings, while prose was generally used by characters of lower social status, for comic or domestic scenes, for letters read out loud, or to indicate mental disturbance.

Verse

By the start of Shakespeare's career, one particular verse metre had come to dominate the language of plays. This was based on a line of ten syllables, arranged so that the beats, or stresses, fell on every second syllable. Thus, each line consisted of five units (or metrical feet), each consisting of an unstressed syllable followed by a stressed one, as follows:

~ /   ~ /   ~ /   ~ /   ~ /

Each of these units is called an iambic foot, and since there are five of them in each line, the metre is called iambic pentameter. Here are two typical examples from the play:

~ / ~ / ~ / ~ / ~ /
To tell | he longs | to see | his son | were strong.　　　　(I.2.34)

~ / ~ / ~ / ~ / ~ /
I am | appoint | ed him | to mur | der you.　　　　(I.2.412)

In the earlier drama of the time, including Shakespeare's first plays, the rhythms of the iambic pentameter tended to be kept very regular, at the risk of becoming monotonous. As Shakespeare's career developed, he became more flexible in his use of the basic metre, incorporating an increasing number of irregularities. Two of the most common variations on the basic iambic pentameter are as follows:

(1) An eleventh, unstressed syllable added to a line, giving what is called a feminine ending:

~ / ~ / ~ / ~ / ~ / ~
How some | times nat | ure will | betray | its foll | y　　　　(I.2.151)

~ / ~ / ~ / ~ / ~ / ~
He's all | my ex | ercise, | my mirth, | my matt | er　　　　(I.2.166)

(2) Reversing the stresses on the first foot of a line, so that it begins with greater emphasis:

/ ~ ~ / ~ / ~ / ~ /
Nothing | but joll | ity. | The gods | themselves　　　　(IV.4.25)

/ ~ ~ / ~ / ~ / ~ /
Sir, you | have done | enough, | and have | performed　　　　(V.1.1)

Sometimes both variations occur in the same line:

/ ~ ~ / ~ / ~ / ~ / ~
Bear the | boy hence; | he shall | not come | about | her.　　　　(II.1.59)

/ ~ ~ / ~ / ~ / ~ / ~
Fancies | too weak | for boys, | too green | and i | dle　　　　(III.2.178)

In passages of dialogue, one verse line can be shared by two speakers. Most editions make this clear by the way the text is set out:

[LEONTES]　　　I might have looked upon my queen's full eyes,
　　　　　　　　Have taken treasure from her lips —
PAULINA　　　　　　　　　　　　　　　　　　And left them
　　　　　　　　More rich for what they yielded.
LEONTES　　　　　　　　　　　　　　　Thou speak'st truth. (V.1.53–55)

Again, in early plays, each verse line tended to be a unit of meaning. Later in his career, Shakespeare much more frequently ran the sense of one line into the next, a technique called enjambement; he also created more heavy breaks in the middle of a line, known as caesuras. Both of these have the effect of obscuring rather than emphasising the underlying rhythm of the lines. Look, for example, at this speech of Leontes, where the frequent use of enjambement, caesura and metrical irregularity all help to destroy the rhythms of the verse and suggest Leontes's disturbed state of mind:

> Nor night nor day no rest. It is but weakness
> To bear the matter thus, mere weakness. If
> The cause were not in being — part o'th'cause,
> She, th'adultress; for the harlot king
> Is quite beyond mine arm, out of the blank
> And level of my brain, plot-proof; but she
> I can hook to me — say that she were gone,
> Given to the fire, a moiety of my rest
> Might come to me again. Who's there? (II.3.1–9)

One verse technique Shakespeare used frequently in his early plays was rhyme. Whole speeches in plays like *Romeo and Juliet* and *A Midsummer Night's Dream* are in rhyming couplets or other rhyming patterns. In later plays Shakespeare confined his use of rhyme to particular groups of characters, such as the witches in *Macbeth*, or to using a couplet to give a special emphasis to the end of a speech or scene.

In *The Winter's Tale*, the basic verse of the play contains absolutely no rhyme at all. Iambic pentameter without any rhymes is called blank verse, and this is the standard verse form of the play. The only use of rhyme in the play is for two particular purposes:

- the songs, which are in a variety of verse forms
- the speech of Time, which is in iambic pentameter and rhyming couplets

If you are writing about the verse of the play, or analysing a speech in verse, you need to beware: do not just describe the features of the verse, but analyse and comment on the effects it creates in the lines you are looking at:

- How do regular, fluid verse rhythms create different effects from irregular, broken ones?
- How might an actor respond to the particular features of the verse in developing his or her character?
- What is different about the way the verse is used by different characters, or by the same characters at different times in the play?
- How does the verse work with other language techniques to create the particular effect of a speech?

Prose

Most of Shakespeare's plays contain sections in prose as well as verse, and *The Winter's Tale* is no exception. As already indicated, prose tended to be given to characters of lower social status, and was used in comic or domestic scenes, for the reading aloud of letters, or to indicate mental disturbance. These categories of prose use do not always apply, however, and it is important to establish the particular effects of prose speeches and scenes in the structure of the play as a whole, especially when prose and verse are mingled as freely as they are in this play.

It is a mistake to think that prose is somehow more naturalistic or realistic than verse. Prose can encompass the language of novels, textbooks, newspapers, magazines, letters, diaries and legal documents, and it can be as structured and artificial as verse. It is the everyday language, in speech and writing, of people of varying degrees of education and literacy, and is consequently infinitely varied in its rhythms, grammatical structures and vocabulary.

In *The Winter's Tale*, the following sections are in prose:

- the opening scene — the conversation between Camillo and Archidamus (I.1)
- the indictment against Hermione (III.2.12–19)
- the dialogue between the Shepherd and the Clown (III.3.58–119)
- the scene between Polixenes and Camillo (IV.2)
- the scene between Autolycus and the Clown (IV.3)
- the entertainments within the sheep-shearing scene (IV.4.181–321) — except for the songs
- most of the conclusion of the scene, from the re-entry of Autolycus (IV.4.574–780) — though the courtly characters, other than Camillo, stick to verse
- the scene between Autolycus and the Gentlemen, Shepherd and Clown (V.2)

For all the above sections of the play, you need to consider a range of issues relating to the use of prose, such as:

- What kind of characters are speaking, and in what context?
- Do these characters use prose throughout the play? If not, why do they use it here?
- What precedes or follows each prose section? Does the prose have the effect of lowering the dramatic temperature after a verse scene? Does it heighten the impact of a verse scene that follows? Or does it simply provide a contrast of tone?
- What kind of prose is it? Is it elaborate, courtly and artificial, or rustic, colloquial and comic? Does it employ long, complex, balanced sentences or short, straightforward ones? What linguistic devices does it employ, and what effects do these create?
- What possibilities for interpretation by the actor are presented by the particular qualities of a prose speech?

Imagery

An *image* is the mental picture conjured up by a particular word or phrase. When writers use related patterns or clusters of images, they are using *imagery* as a literary technique. Such imagery may serve a number of purposes: it may be a feature of characterisation, infusing characters with particular associations; it may contribute to the creation of mood and atmosphere; or it may support the thematic significance of the text.

Shakespeare uses highly wrought, complex imagery throughout his plays. A particular pattern of imagery will often imbue a play with its own distinctive atmosphere. For example, in *Macbeth*, the language persistently harps on *blood*. The word itself crops up continually, together with variations such as *bloody* or *bleeding*, related words such as *gory*, and an emphasis on the colour *red*. Working alongside equally evocative imagery of *physical violence*, *night*, *darkness* and *the supernatural*, the effect created is not difficult to grasp.

It can be misleading to generalise about Shakespeare's imagery, but it is useful to recognise the broad contrast in its use between the tragedies and the comedies.

- In the tragedies, the imagery tends to create unpleasant emotive associations. *Violence, blood, disease, darkness, evil* and *the supernatural, lust* and *appetite* walk hand in hand with images of *wild animals, winter weather* and *storm and tempest*.
- In the comedies, the overriding images are of *love* and *friendship, spring flowers, birds, calm weather, good health* and *spirituality*, with a particular emphasis on *song, dance* and *music*.

When it comes to the last plays, one striking aspect of their imagery is the way it combines the characteristic images of the tragedies and comedies. Images of *disease* and *cure, winter* and *spring, youth* and *old age, tempest* and *music* work side by side, suggesting a more inclusive and balanced view of life. All of these opposing image clusters are employed in *The Winter's Tale* as well as the other romances, and seem appropriate for plays that deal in the mode of tragicomedy.

In studying the play, you would do well to focus on the following key image clusters, giving careful consideration to the effects they create:

- disease and cure
- sleep, sleeplessness and dreams
- the seasons and weather
- birds, animals and flowers
- storm and tempest
- time
- grace and graciousness
- the gods
- nature and natural processes
- art and the artificial

- music, song and dance
- youth and old age

When we watch and listen to a performance of the play, we are probably not consciously aware of such verbal patterning, but it will nevertheless be helping to condition our response. Furthermore, aspects of the imagery are likely to have been taken into account in the design and staging of the production, so that set and costumes, lighting, music and sound effects may well be enhancing the play's linguistic features. Closer reading and study of the text will reveal some of these verbal features in more detail, enabling us to assess their impact at a more consciously analytical level. In writing about imagery, it is therefore important not merely to note image patterns, but to consider the effects they create on our response to the play.

(See also sample essay 1 (pages 125–27), which gives an account of some principal features of the play's imagery.)

Structure

The structure of *The Winter's Tale* is bold and clear, almost symphonic in its creation of three movements, each with its own particular mood, but with echoes of the others interwoven throughout. The first movement, consisting of Acts I–III, is a bold and passionate statement of Leontes's irrational jealousy that sows the seeds for the pastoral second movement in its final scene of the baby's rescue by shepherds. The low-key beginning of Act IV, the second movement, is soon succeeded by the celebratory mood of the sheep-shearing festival, with Autolycus and Perdita as its contrasting presiding spirits. Echoes of the first movement emerge in Polixenes's violent anger, but there are enough hints of a positive resolution to prevent this from being the dominant mood. Act V, the play's third and final movement, is subdued, steeped in an air of spiritual sadness that develops into the transcendental joys of forgiveness and reconciliation. As in a symphony, leitmotifs from all the previous movements recur here.

These three movements are unequal in length, and in modern productions the play is usually performed in two parts, with an interval after Act III. We do not know whether intervals were taken at outdoor theatres such as the Globe, though many plays of the period do build up to a point about three-fifths of the way through that seems designed for such a break. In *The Winter's Tale* this coincides with the play's 'wide gap of time', and Time's chorus is a striking and apt way to pick up the story after an intermission.

Structuring of plays at the indoor Blackfriars, however, demanded a different dramatic framework, with regular breaks needed to trim the candles that lit the theatre. The five-act structure familiar from printed play texts probably developed

to serve this need; indeed, there is evidence that some of the King's Men's existing plays were revised to this end when they began to perform at the Blackfriars, one example being Shakespeare's *Measure for Measure*, which was probably restructured by Thomas Middleton.

Shakespeare carefully subdivides the opening movement of *The Winter's Tale* to cater for the five-act structure. With the first scene as a kind of prologue, Act I provides the play's exposition, setting up Leontes's jealousy and preparing the ground for his confrontation with Hermione. In Act II, we find Leontes in conflict with all around him, from Hermione to Paulina, Antigonus and the lords, reaching a climax in the removal of the baby to be exposed to its fate. Act III focuses on Hermione's trial and its dramatic conclusion, but is framed by two quite different scenes — the calm description of the oracle and the storm-tossed arrival of the baby on the Bohemian coast, with the destruction of the agents of its exposure and its rescue by the Shepherd and Clown.

Acts IV and V are also structured and paced carefully within themselves. Act IV, for example, begins with an unexpected chorus that makes way for the rather flatly written scene between Polixenes and Camillo, which is engineered deliberately to enhance the impact of Autolycus's freewheeling incursion into the action. And Act V scene 1 builds carefully towards the play's anticipated denouement, only to toy with the audience in the anticlimactic discussion between the three Gentlemen in order to heighten the surprise ending. Perhaps the only moment in the play when Shakespeare's pacing falters is at the end of Act IV scene 4, when Florizel and Perdita's escape plans take a disproportionate amount of time to establish, which dissipates the dramatic tension that has been built up.

The play, then, has a number of alternative structures layered one on top of another: two parts, three movements, five acts, and each act carefully structured with its own dramatic shape geared to the rhythms of the whole play.

Themes

The themes of a literary text may or may not have been developed consciously by the author. Usually, we have no means of knowing an author's intentions; what is important is the impact of the text on a reader or, in the case of a play, an audience. Even if an author has written explicitly about the thematic content of a work, that does not preclude other themes from coming to the attention of particular readers. It can even happen that a text unconsciously undermines its author's professed themes: in *Moll Flanders*, for example, Daniel Defoe seems to relish the sexual immorality he is ostensibly attacking, while in *To Kill a Mockingbird*, Harper Lee's portrayal of the black characters sometimes employs elements of the very racial stereotyping that the novel aims to expose.

Responding to the themes of a complex drama such as *The Winter's Tale* is not as simple as asking what the 'moral' of the play is. The themes range across personal relationships, social structures, religious and political morality and philosophical reflections on the meaning of life; they are developed through a web of overlapping and interconnecting ideas, and are made evident through plot and narrative, characterisation, language and imagery.

Personal themes

The first kind of relationship brought to our attention in the play is the **friendship** between Leontes and Polixenes, which began in their boyhood. In talking to Hermione, Polixenes stresses the innocence of their friendship, suggesting that this was in some way compromised by their subsequent relationships with women (I.2.76–80). Leontes, however, identifies Hermione's acceptance of his marriage proposal, after three months' delay, as equal in value to her success in persuading Polixenes to extend his visit to Sicilia (I.2.88–105). **Marriage** is thus balanced against friendship — two of the cornerstones of human relationships. Therefore, as Polixenes points out, when Leontes believes that he and Hermione have been engaged in an adulterous affair, his sense of **betrayal** must inevitably be exacerbated (I.2.451–57). The theme of betrayal is developed further, particularly in the behaviour of Camillo in both parts of the play.

Leontes's mistrust of his wife and friend is mistaken, however. His suspicions are motivated by inexplicable psychological disturbance and his **jealousy** becomes the key theme of the play's first movement: its effects spread far beyond his circle of family and friends to have political repercussions in depriving Sicilia of an heir to the throne and damaging its relations with Bohemia. Shakespeare forcefully portrays the personal costs of jealousy, not just on Leontes's innocent wife and children but on Leontes himself, as he descends into barely coherent rage and paranoia. The destructive power of his jealousy is thrown into relief by the sexual rivalry of Mopsa and Dorcas, which revisits the theme in comic mode and in a minor key.

Other relationships in the play are designed to present further contrasts with Leontes's irrational treatment of his wife. The marriage of Paulina and Antigonus, though characterised by Leontes as the stereotype of shrewish wife and hen-pecked husband, seems to be based on mutual respect, and she is still mourning his loss 16 years after his death (see V.3.132–35). We also hear of the Shepherd's marriage, when he reminisces generously and affectionately about his wife's skills in domestic management and hospitality.

In total contrast, the practical business of marriage is set against the idealism of **love**, as seen in the relationship of Florizel and Perdita. Their love overrides all other considerations, whether of family, social class differences, or political concerns. Both express their love in language of striking poetic beauty, and it is their **constancy** that is perhaps most impressive: when disaster strikes, Florizel claims his love is merely 'delayed, | But nothing altered' (IV.4.442–43), while Perdita responds to Camillo's suggestion that love is altered by 'affliction' with the firm statement that 'affliction may subdue the cheek, | But not take in the mind' (IV.4.551–56). Later, Florizel asserts that their ill fortune has 'power no jot | [...] to change our loves' (V.1.215–17).

Love is one of the agents of the play's positive outcome; the other is Leontes's **repentance**. At the end of Act III scene 2 he promises that daily penance at the tomb of his wife and son will be his 'recreation' (III.2.235–39), and re-creation indeed turns out to be what his 16 years of 'saint-like sorrow' (V.1.2) achieve. Cleomenes thinks he has done enough, that he has redeemed all his faults and offered more penitence than his sins merited (V.1.1–6), a sentiment later echoed by Camillo (V.3.49–53), but the sight of Hermione's statue has 'conjured to remembrance' his 'evils' (V.3.40), confirming his continued penitence. Cleomenes told him that he needed to 'forgive' himself (V.1.6), but it is Hermione's **forgiveness** that his self-abasement before her statue — 'I am ashamed' (V.3.37) — earns him. Her forgiveness is made explicit not in words but in her embracing him (V.3.111), and her restoration to life is the concluding element in the play's denouement, which is one of **reconciliation** between those who were split apart, both physically and emotionally, by Leontes's jealousy.

Social and political themes

The play sets up an opposition between **court and country**, something Shakespeare had explored previously, notably in *As You Like It*. On the face of it, the Sicilian court seems to be presented as a claustrophobic hotbed of festering passions and tyrannous rule, while rural Bohemia is portrayed as a life-affirming, celebratory environment in which generosity and love can flourish. Examined more closely, however, the play's two worlds are more complex than this: the world of the court contains notable examples of courage and virtue, and that of the country is marred by jealousy, dishonesty and ignorance. As a princess raised to be a shepherdess, Perdita is a symbolic embodiment of the best of both worlds, though had she not turned out to be a princess the proposed marital union of court and country would have been socially unthinkable.

This raises the issue of **social class**, which is made explicit principally in Polixenes's attitude to his son's relationship with a shepherdess. Though he and Camillo both recognise Perdita's innate qualities — she is 'of most rare note' (IV.2.33–34), with 'Nothing she does or seems | But smacks of something greater than herself' (IV.4.157–58) — her low social status is enough for her to be classified contemptuously as 'a sheep-hook' (IV.4.399) who is 'Worthy enough a herdsman' (IV.4.414). Leontes's reaction to Perdita is interesting: he laments that Florizel's 'choice is not so rich in worth as beauty' (V.1.213), as if 'worth' were a quality reserved for those of elevated social status, yet he still goes on to express his own sexual attraction towards her (V.1.222–23).

Within these assumptions about class, the rise of the Shepherd's family is an interesting illustration of the possibility of upward social mobility in Elizabethan and Jacobean England, first through their acquisition of wealth and finally through the courtly patronage that raises them to the gentry. Autolycus, conversely, illustrates the dangers of a descent in the social scale, in his decline from his status as a member of the prince's retinue to the level of a 'masterless man' obliged to live by begging and criminal behaviour.

It is essentially social class issues that lead to the employment of **deception and disguise** in the case of both Florizel and Autolycus — the former to pursue a socially unacceptable affair, the latter to pursue his life of crime in order to survive at the lowest level of society. Deceptions of various kinds drive the plot in other areas too, notably in Paulina's 16-year fiction of Hermione's death, culminating in one of the play's most elaborate disguises — that of queen-as-statue. All of these elements contribute to one of the themes most persistently explored throughout Shakespeare's plays, the difference between **appearance and reality**.

On the political level, deception also raises the issues of **loyalty and betrayal**. Loyalty to one's sovereign was paramount, but when it came into conflict with a higher morality, the consequence was an ethical dilemma such as that in which Camillo is placed by Leontes's demand that he murder Polixenes, and Antigonus by the cruel mission he is enjoined by oath to carry out. Camillo is faced with further conflicts of loyalty later in the play when Polixenes refuses his request to return to Sicilia, and his subsequent actions might be judged as a betrayal of both the king and the prince, despite their positive outcome. Leontes is obsessed with his courtiers' failed loyalty, calling them a 'nest of traitors' (II.3.81), but Paulina turns his accusation back against him, suggesting the only traitor is 'himself' (II.3.83). In standing up against him, Paulina and the lords paradoxically demonstrate their loyalty, and just as Camillo becomes indispensable to Polixenes (IV.2.8–16), so Paulina stands in a parallel position with Leontes, who admits to the 'great comfort' (V.3.1) her service has given him. Even Autolycus maintains a kind of residual loyalty to Florizel, whom he persists in referring to as 'the prince my master' (IV.4.774), though his motives are clearly more self-serving, and he ends up relying on the Clown to restore him to Florizel's good graces (V.2.126–27).

Religious and philosophical themes

The opposition between court and country finds more abstract expression in the debate between the relative merits of **Art and Nature**, a subject of much interest in Shakespeare's time which may seem rather academic to us today. However, as articulated in the discussion between Perdita and Polixenes on the ethical accept-ability of grafting, the debate relates directly to modern anxieties about such issues as genetic modification, cloning and stem cell research, with their emotive language of 'Frankenstein foods' and 'designer babies'. Nature seems to be one of the play's presiding deities. It is invoked by Paulina as 'good goddess Nature' (II.3.103) and by Perdita as 'great creating nature' (IV.4.88), but as Polixenes points out, there is no art that 'adds to nature' that is not in itself 'an art | That nature makes'; thus 'The art itself is nature' (IV.4.88–97). Ultimately, the play seems to endorse Polixenes's viewpoint, with its statue scene that represents a complex interaction of art, even invoking the name of the supposed sculptor, Julio Romano (V.2.77), and nature. The scene is also, of course, a piece of theatre — an art that, according to Hamlet, holds 'the mirror up to nature' (*Hamlet*, III.2.22).

Few would interpret *The Winter's Tale* as an explicitly Christian play, least of all in any narrow doctrinal sense. It owes as much to Greek mythology and pagan fertility rituals as it does to any specific relationship with the official orthodoxy of Jacobean Protestantism, though there are occasional Christian references placed carefully in its pre-Christian world, such as allusions to original sin and Judas's betrayal of Jesus. In the broadest sense, though, **religion** plays a key role in the overall scheme of the play. The play's structure is partly based on the Christian patterning of sin, penance and redemption, and one of its most frequently used words is 'grace', suggesting the divine blessings granted to those who lead holy lives. The word is often spoken by, or associated with, Hermione, whose 'resurrection' has overtones of Christian belief, and its derivatives, 'gracious' and 'disgrace', are also used in the play. There is a sense of sacred ritual in Cleomenes and Dion's account of the oracle and in the statue scene, while Paulina's injunction to the assembled company, 'It is required | You do awake your faith' (V.3.94–95), sets the seal on the play's religious suggestiveness.

Time is also a central preoccupation of the play, not just in its personification as chorus, but in its persistent evocation through various strands of the imagery. Units of time mentioned vary from the 'hours [and] minutes' that, according to Leontes, illicit lovers wish to pass more swiftly (I.2.289–90) to the 'Nine changes of the wat'ry star' (I.2.1) of Polixenes's visit and Hermione's pregnancy; from the 16-year 'wide gap of time' (V.3.154) covered by the play's narrative, to the Shepherd's 'fourscore three' years of age (IV.4.432). We are also taken back in time 'twenty-three years' (I.2.155) to the childhood friendship of Leontes and Polixenes, and forward to the concept of 'perpetuity' (I.2.5). Time is implicit too in the play's seasonal imagery with its reference to the natural cycles of birth, growth, death and renewal, highlighted by the allusion to the myth of Proserpina (IV.4.116). Ultimately, it is the cyclical nature of human life that the play invokes, both morally and physically. Time deals out 'both joy and terror | Of good and bad [and] makes and unfolds error' (IV.1.1–2); it also determines the repetitive process by which 'things dying' are succeeded by 'things new born' (III.3.100–01). No wonder Leontes asks Paulina to 'Hastily lead away' at the end of the play (V.3.155), in his anxiety to enjoy what has been restored to him before time can revoke its gifts.

The play in performance

Simon Forman

Simon Forman was a fascinating figure in Jacobean London. An astrologer and quack doctor, he lived his life on the fringes of scandal and intrigue, and died while rowing across the Thames in September 1611.

In the last months of his life, Forman's theatre-going took him at least four times to the Globe, where he saw not only *The Winter's Tale* but *Cymbeline*, *Macbeth* and a non-Shakespearean version of the life of Richard II. His notes on the performances are often rather garbled, but essentially he gives a general plot summary and occasionally draws moral lessons 'for common policy', as he says in the heading to his accounts.

His description of *The Winter's Tale*, which he saw on 15 May 1611, repays close attention. Here it is in full, with the spelling modernised and the punctuation amended to make it slightly more coherent.

> Observe there how Leontes, the king of Sicilia, was overcome with jealousy of his wife with the king of Bohemia, his friend that came to see him; and how he contrived his death and would have had his cup-bearer to have poisoned [him], who gave the king of Bohemia warning thereof, and fled with him to Bohemia.
>
> Remember also how he sent to the oracle of Apollo, and the answer of Apollo that she was guiltless and that the king was jealous etc; and how, except the child was found again that was lost, the king should die without issue: for the child was carried into Bohemia and there laid in a forest and brought up by a shepherd. And the king of Bohemia's son married that wench, and how they fled into Sicilia to Leontes; and the shepherd having showed the letter of the nobleman by whom Leontes sent away that child, and the jewels found about her, she was known to be Leontes's daughter, and was then 16 years old.
>
> Remember also the rogue that came in all tattered like colt-pixie, and how he feigned him sick and to have been robbed of all that he had and how he cozened the poor man of all his money, and after came to the sheep-shear[ing] with a pedlar's pack, and there cozened them again of all their money; and how he changed apparel with the king of Bohemia's son, and then how he turned courtier etc.
>
> Beware of trusting feigned beggars or fawning fellows.

This is a tantalising but frustrating account. Forman makes no mention of the bear or the statue scene, both of which might have been expected to elicit a strong response. Instead of commenting on what, to us, are the play's central themes of forgiveness and reconciliation, he draws a limited practical moral only from the activities of Autolycus. But then, Forman was not a theatre critic: such people were unknown until the next century; and his accounts seem to have been intended only for himself. We must be content with this tantalising glimpse of how the play was first staged.

Performance history

Forman saw *The Winter's Tale* at the Globe; the general assumption is that it also played at the indoor Blackfriars, though there is no conclusive evidence of this. We do know, however, that it was performed seven times at court, presumably by royal command, before 1640 and the outbreak of the English Civil War. This shows that it was popular with courtly audiences, but we have no way of knowing if its popularity was more general.

It was not, however, one of the plays of Shakespeare that was revived in adapted form when the theatres reopened with the restoration of Charles II to the monarchy in 1660. Its next recorded stage performances were not until 1741, sandwiched between the two halves of a concert, and later, embellished by a 'Grand Ballet', at Covent Garden in 1742. Subsequently, in common with other Shakespeare plays, it was performed only in bastardised versions, focusing on the jollity and spectacle of the sheep-shearing scene, surrounded by varying amounts of the rest of the play — sometimes none of it at all. Even its title became *Florizel and Perdita; or The Sheep Shearing*.

David Garrick, the actor and theatre manager, put on a three-act version in 1756, which gained much approval. In the prologue, he speaks of 'the five long acts from which our three are taken' and claims that the 'precious liquor' of Shakespeare's genius in the original play is now 'confined and bottled for your taste'. A friend wrote to him that he had given 'an elegant form to a monstrous composition', and his own performance as Leontes, though based only on Act V of the original, was much admired.

More of Shakespeare's play was restored in the nineteenth century, though the taste for elaborate productions with enormous casts and stunning scenic spectacle did not allow for anything like a complete text. The role of Leontes attracted most of the great actor-managers of the nineteenth-century theatre, such as John Philip Kemble and William Charles Macready, while Sarah Siddons was a notable Hermione. Charles Kean's 1856 production, crammed with Grecian spectacle, ran for 102 consecutive performances. Mary Anderson's 1887 production began the intermittent tradition of doubling Hermione and Perdita, in which roles she herself was highly praised. Even then, she could write in her preface to the acting edition of her version that large cuts to the original text were 'unavoidable' since 'no audience of these days would desire to have *The Winter's Tale* produced in its entirety'.

The early twentieth century saw a dramatic revolution in attitudes to Shakespearean production, exemplified by Harley Granville Barker, who not only restored the original text for his 1912 production but eschewed elaborate settings and spectacle so that the play could run uninterrupted by scene changes, working in much the same way as it might have done at the Globe or the Blackfriars. The critics either loved it or hated it.

Productions since the start of the twentieth century have been legion, restoring the play to popularity with audiences and attracting notable directors such as the legendary Peter Brook, and great star actors such as John Gielgud, who played Leontes in Brook's 1951 production.

Modern interpretations

The fairy-tale quality of *The Winter's Tale* has led many recent directors to update its setting to a variety of different periods, finding a range of cultural resonances and contemporary analogues in an attempt to recreate the play's impact for a modern audience.

In 1969, at the height of the 'swinging sixties', Trevor Nunn's RSC production dressed Leontes's court in the latest Carnaby Street fashions, and imagined the sheep-shearing festivities as a hippy festival with rock music settings for Autolycus's songs. The opening scene was presented in all-white décor in a child's nursery, giving concrete form to the talk of childhood and a touching centrality to the doomed Mamillius. The jealousy of Barrie Ingham's Leontes was marked by a dramatic change of lighting in which we actually saw the upstage figures of Hermione and Polixenes acting out his deranged fantasies. The theme of regeneration was emphasised by Judi Dench's doubling of Hermione and Perdita, necessitating some clever manipulation of the final scene. The theatre critic Milton Shulman, however, suggested that Shakespeare would have had 'hilarious hysterics' at the interpretation of 'this popular nonsense as some profound allegory about a search for love through suffering and ultimate redemption'. Even as late as 1969, he was not alone in refusing to take the play seriously.

One major decision for directors and designers is how to create the contrast between Sicilia and Bohemia. In Adrian Noble's 1992 production at Stratford, John Nettles's Leontes presided over a 1930s court of elegant, gauze-draped spaces, while the sheep-shearing became an old-fashioned village fete, with street band, bunting and trestle tables. However, Noble used a recurring visual image to tie the two worlds together: in the opening scene, brightly-coloured balloons floated over the court celebrations; later, Time's speech drifted down on a stray balloon to be read by Camillo; Richard McCabe's music-hall Autolycus also descended from above, attached to a massive bunch of green balloons; and the sexual equipment of each of the dancing satyrs was partly represented by a pair of balloons. Key moments were enhanced by a powerful sense of emblematic stage spectacle. A tremendous storm broke out as Leontes defied the oracle in the trial scene, blowing the courtiers' umbrellas across the stage. And the realistic bear was about to snap up the tasty morsel of the baby Perdita when the sudden descent of a phantasm of Hermione, in billowing silks, drove it away.

In Gregory Doran's RSC production of 1999, Sicilia had taken a further step back in time, to the Edwardian period, with hints of the mythical kingdom of Ruritania in the court of Antony Sher's Leontes. As the critic Nicholas de Jongh pointed out, this was a period 'when rigid traditionalists faced new threats of feminism and sexual liberation'. The strict codes of the court were given visual representation in the strait-laced dress of wing collars, morning suits and monocles, in a court stuffed with both pompous ritual and whispering innuendo. Sher, who had researched particular medical conditions as the basis of Leontes's mental state, fell backwards as if convulsed when his jealousy struck, hitting the floor with such violence that the audience gasped. They gasped, too, at Alexandra Gilbreath's appearance as Hermione in the trial scene, genuinely looking as if she had spent weeks starving in a narrow cell. Regeneration was marked in this production by the resurrection of Emily Bruni's crippled, wheelchair-bound Mamillius in the form of a sprightly Perdita. For the critic Georgina Brown, this made 'poignant dramatic sense', but Paul Taylor felt it counteracted the sense of Mamillius's death 'as a tragedy time cannot redeem'. Thirty years after Shulman's dismissal of the play, John Gross was now commenting that it 'is so much a romance, so easily discussed in terms of ritual and symbol, that it is easy to forget how much realistic drama takes place within the fairy-tale confines of the plot'.

It was again realism rather than fairy-tale or ritual that was stressed in the first two major productions of the twenty-first century. In Nicholas Hytner's 2001 National Theatre production, the play was brought bang up to date, with Alex Jennings's Leontes presiding over a corporate empire in the penthouse suite of a high-rise office block. A huge photograph of Leontes and Polixenes as children, dirty-kneed in their school rugby kit, hung on the wall, while the king's smart-casual designer clothes were in ironic contrast to his obsessive outbursts. Bohemia, meanwhile, had turned into a Glastonbury-style pop festival, with Phil Daniels playing Autolycus in the style of Ali G. None of this diminished the play's emotional power, and the reunited mother and daughter remained on stage at the end, in Paul Taylor's words, 'clutching each other like shipwreck survivors'. The following year the RSC returned to the play, taking it back in time again — this time to 1940s America, its powerful political leaders presented as a cross between business tycoons and gangsters, and the square-dancing Bohemians redolent of the musical *Oklahoma!*

That the play has survived such a diverse range of presentations is a testimony to Shakespeare's immense dramatic skill, frequently acknowledged by reviewers. In 2001, Nicholas de Jongh found that 'the superlative magic of the finale [worked] exhilarating wonders once again', while in 1999 Charles Spencer admitted:

> If I were forced to save only one Shakespeare play, I think my hand would
> hover over *Hamlet* and *King Lear* before finally opting for *The Winter's Tale*.

Critical debate

The concept of Shakespeare's plays as objects of critical scrutiny did not really emerge until the eighteenth century. Earlier commentators, such as Tate, Davenant and Dryden, were often concerned with rationalising and justifying their own adaptations of Shakespearean texts. Dryden, whose Shakespearean rewrites included *Troilus and Cressida*, *Antony and Cleopatra* (as *All for Love*) and *The Tempest* (*The Enchanted Island*), found the plot of *The Winter's Tale* 'grounded in impossibilities'.

The gradually developing notion of Shakespeare's greatness led some critics to dismiss the plays they didn't like as either apprentice works, products of Shakespeare's dotage or the result of collaborations with inferior dramatists. Alexander Pope, for example, in 1725, considered little of *The Winter's Tale* to be Shakespeare's.

With the Romantic period, in the early nineteenth century, came concepts of Shakespeare's genius, like some kind of inexplicable natural force, plus a closer examination of his use of language. At various times since then, the focus of Shakespearean criticism has been on his stagecraft, his delineation of character and psychology, the mythic resonances of his plays and his use of imagery.

Criticism of *The Winter's Tale* has frequently seen it as part of the group of Shakespeare's final plays. Victorian critics often saw these works as exhibiting a serenity and tranquillity suggestive of a mellowing Shakespeare in semi-retirement. For some early twentieth-century critics, however, they demonstrated Shakespeare's boredom with drama and his interest only in fanciful poetry. Neither of these views survives even a cursory study of the actual plays, and while the later assessment of them as experimental seems nearer to the truth, some critics have used this term as a sort of excuse for their perceived inadequacies.

Perhaps critical assessments of Shakespeare's plays tell us more about the critics than about the plays. Critical theory has now become a bewildering web of conflicting orthodoxies in which not only the text but students too may get left behind. While many A-level examiners promote a kind of liberal humanist approach to literature which prioritises an informed personal response stemming from close textual scrutiny, the specifications now emphasise the contextualisation of texts both in the historical, social and political climate that produced them, and in the critical debate of succeeding ages.

Modern critical approaches can shed considerable light on the play. For example, **political criticism**, which might include **Marxist** analysis and **New Historicism**, reminds us that literary texts are products of a particular set of socio-political circumstances from which they cannot be divorced, and that they are informed by a range of cultural preoccupations and anxieties that manifest themselves whether they are consciously intended by the writer or not. Politics plays more of a role in *The Winter's Tale* than is often recognised, for example in the portrait of two kings whose use and abuse of power forces them to confront issues of succession, responsible government and international alliances which would be familiar to a Jacobean audience.

Feminist criticism, similarly, challenges assumptions about gender and exposes both the sexual stereotyping embodied in a text and the way in which such stereotypes might be subverted. Whether Shakespeare's plays exhibit feminist sympathies, or whether they merely accept and endorse the patriarchal status quo and the misogyny of their time, is an issue that can only enhance a consideration of the roles of Hermione, Paulina and Perdita.

Other critical ideologies focus on language rather than social and historical context, and are based on complex issues of linguistic philosophy that can make them difficult for a non-specialist to grasp. **Structuralism** and **post-structuralism** see the relationship between language and meaning (or signifier and signified) as essentially fluid and shifting, revealing contradiction and ambivalence to such a degree that interpretation becomes no more than an identification of an ever-expanding range of possible meanings. In this context, as Roland Barthes suggests, the role of the author is irrelevant, and any concept of authorial intention or control is a mere chimera. What this does not mean, however, is that a text can mean anything we want it to.

Deconstruction is a broad term, but its adherents are particularly adept at interrogating texts to find their contradictions and ambiguities, their generic discontinuities and their revealing gaps and silences. Deconstructionist critics often arrive at challenging and controversial interpretations which may seem perverse but have the merit of sending us back to the text to question it for ourselves.

Performance criticism looks at how the form of dramatic texts is determined by their basis in theatrical practice, examining them against what is known of the original stage conditions for which they were produced and the way they have been represented subsequently in other theatres and performance media. This approach questions the notion of a definitive text and undermines the concept of authorship, as theatre is essentially collaborative and ephemeral.

In practice, most critical analysis, including your own, is a synthesis of different critical methods and ideologies.

The following quotations represent a range of critical approaches to the play:

> The calm, regular, classical beauty of Hermione's character is the more impressive from the wild and Gothic accompaniments of her story, and the beautiful relief afforded by the pastoral and romantic grace which is thrown around her daughter Perdita. (Anna Jameson, 1832)

The sudden jealousy of Leontes, though unaccountable, is not impossible. [...] Except Autolycus, none of the characters show much of Shakespeare's philosophic depth. (Hartley Coleridge, 1851)

It has all the licence and it has all the charm of a fairy tale. (Arthur Symons, 1890)

When Hermione descends from the pedestal into her husband's arms, the impossibility of reconciliation is passed by in silence, and Leontes busies himself in finding a husband for the aged and unattractive Paulina. (Robert Bridges, 1907)

But why introduce that bear? [...] Why [...] not engulf Antigonus with the rest — or, better still, as he tries to row aboard? I can discover no answer to that. If anyone ask my private opinion [...] it is that the Bear-Pit in Southwark, hard by the Globe Theatre, had a tame animal to let out, and the Globe management took the opportunity to make a popular hit. (Arthur Quiller-Couch, 1918)

It is difficult to resist the conclusion that [Shakespeare] was getting bored himself. Bored with people, bored with real life, bored with drama, bored, in fact, with everything except poetry and poetical dreams. (Lytton Strachey, 1922)

Pastoral is never to be mistaken for a transcript of rustic life. Its significance resides not in any fidelity to the fact of the peasant but in its relation to the state of mind of the world-wearied courtier or scholar who writes it. (E. K. Chambers, 1925)

Shakespeare blends the realistic and the symbolic with the surest touch. [...] Perdita [...] is one of Shakespeare's richest characters; at once a symbol and a human being. (E. M. W. Tillyard, 1938)

Shakespeare disappoints our expectation in one important respect. The recognition of Leontes and his daughter takes place off stage; we only hear three gentlemen talking prose about it [...], and are denied the satisfaction of such a scene as we might have supposed would crown the play. (Mark Van Doren, 1939)

Hermione, then, comes back from the dead, and the hushed and gracious verse of the statue scene speaks of the resurrection of the Christian to eternal life here and hereafter. (S. L. Bethell, 1956)

Shakespeare's stage-craft in this play is [...] novel, subtle and revolutionary. (Nevill Coghill, 1958)

The play is about the process of social change in 17th-century England: the division between court and country, the mastery of nature by the arts of man, the toughness of traditional rural life in the face of political change, the hope for a regenerated England through a reunion of court with cottage, the acceptance of the processes of history. (Charles Barber, 1964)

The morals of silence are as unstable in *The Winter's Tale* as time itself. The eloquence of Hermione and Paulina contrasts with the cowardly silence of Leontes's courtiers. (Juliet Dusinberre, 1975)

The ending of *The Winter's Tale* is not [...] a vision of ultimate unity. The emphasis is not on the social group but on the individuals whose sufferings we have closely followed. [They] must salvage what they can. (Stanley Wells, 1988)

If through Hermione Shakespeare exposes contradictions in male attitudes to women, through Paulina he demystifies the stereotype of the scold. (Bill Overton, 1989)

Like the tragedies, *The Winter's Tale* shows us how terrible is the human capacity to destroy. The play is not a tragedy, however, for it gives as much emphasis to healing and renewal as it does to destruction. It displays the power of Faith and asserts its marriage with Art. (Susan L. Powell, 1995)

Useful quotations

Whether or not you are allowed to have your text with you in an exam, it is useful to have learned a range of quotations covering various aspects of the play. The best quotations to learn are those that could be used to illustrate more than one area. Consider the usefulness of the quotations selected below in terms of what they might show about character, themes, language, imagery or dramatic effect.

Act I scene 1

I think there is not in the world either malice or matter to alter it.
(*Archidamus complacently assesses Polixenes and Leontes's friendship*)

Act I scene 2

We were as twinned lambs that did frisk i'th'sun | And bleat the one at th'other. (*Polixenes describes childhood innocence in pastoral terms*)

Too hot, too hot! | To mingle friendship far is mingling bloods. | I have tremor cordis on me: my heart dances, | But not for joy, not joy. (*Leontes is struck by jealousy*)

He makes a July's day short as December, | And with his varying childness cures in me | Thoughts that would thick my blood. (*Polixenes talks of his son in terms of two of the play's key images*)

Many thousand on's | Have the disease and feel't not. (*Leontes finds comfort in the fact that he is not alone*)

Good my lord, be cured | Of this diseased opinion. (*Camillo urges Leontes to think again*)

Were my wife's liver | Infected as her life, she would not live | The running of one glass. (*Leontes continues to talk in terms of an infectious disease*)

If I could find example | Of thousands that had struck anointed kings | And flourished after, I'd not do't. (*Camillo takes the moral high ground*)

O then my best blood turn | To an infected jelly. (*Polixenes denies adultery with Hermione*)

Act II scene 1

A sad tale's best for winter. (*Mamillius prepares to entertain his mother before his own sad tale overtakes him*)

I must be patient till the heavens look | With an aspect more favourable. (*Hermione demonstrates restraint*)

This action I now go on | Is for my better grace. (Hermione finds positive value in suffering)

Act II scene 2

There is no lady living | So meet for this great errand. (*Emilia expresses faith in Paulina*)

This child was prisoner to the womb, and is | By law and process of great nature thence | Freed and enfranchised. (*Paulina persuades the Gaoler to release the baby*)

Act II scene 3

Nor night nor day no rest. (*Leontes laments his lack of sleep*)

I come to bring him sleep. (*Paulina promises to restore Leontes's rest*)

It is an heretic that makes the fire, | Not she which burns in't. (*Paulina scorns Leontes's threats*)

Shall I live on to see this bastard kneel | And call me father? (*Leontes forcefully rejects paternity*)

Come on, poor babe; | Some powerful spirit instruct the kites and ravens | To be thy nurses! (*Antigonus invokes supernatural protection for the child*)

Act III scene 1

The climate's delicate, the air most sweet, | Fertile the isle, the temple much surpassing | The common praise it bears. (*Cleomenes describes Delphos*)

...gracious be the issue! (*Dion prays for a positive outcome*)

Act III scene 2

...if powers divine | Behold our human actions, as they do, | I doubt not then but innocence shall make | False accusation blush, and tyranny | Tremble at patience. (*Hermione predicts divine retribution*)

Sir, spare your threats. | The bug which you would fright me with, I seek. (*Hermione embraces the prospect of death*)

Now, my liege, | Tell me what blessings I have here alive | That I should fear to die. (*Hermione offers a realistic assessment of her position*)

There is no truth at all i'th'oracle! | The sessions shall proceed: this is mere falsehood. (*Leontes makes his biggest mistake*)

A thousand knees, | Ten thousand years together, naked, fasting, | Upon a barren mountain, and still winter | In storm perpetual, could not move the gods | To look that way thou wert. (*Paulina asserts that no amount of penitence will gain Leontes divine forgiveness*)

Once a day I'll visit | The chapel where they lie, and tears shed there | Shall be my recreation. (*Leontes promises daily penance*)

Act III scene 3

In my conscience, | The heavens with that we have in hand are angry | And frown upon's. (*The Mariner blames the storm on divine anger*)

Blossom, speed thee well! (*Antigonus anticipates Perdita's association with flowers*)

Thou met'st with things dying, I with things new born. (*The Shepherd marks the play's turning point*)

Act IV scene 1

Impute it not a crime | To me or my swift passage that I slide | O'er sixteen years. (*Time apologises for passing over such a long period*)

Act IV scene 2

Better not to have had thee than thus to want thee. (*Polixenes comments on Camillo's indispensability*)

I have heard, sir, of such a man, who hath a daughter of most rare note. (*Camillo shares rumours of Perdita*)

Act IV scene 3

...the red blood reigns in the winter's pale. (*Autolycus's song embodies the new mood of the play*)

...a snapper-up of unconsidered trifles. (*Autolycus describes his occupation*)

Act IV scene 4

Apprehend | Nothing but jollity. [...] let's be red with mirth. (*Florizel spreads good cheer*)

Come, quench your blushes and present yourself | That which you are, Mistress o'th'Feast. (*The Shepherd demands that Perdita should play her role*)

…well you fit our ages | With flowers of winter. (*Polixenes accepts the appropriateness of Perdita's bouquet*)

Sir, the year growing ancient, | Not yet on summer's death nor on the birth | Of trembling winter… (*Perdita defines the season*)

…I have heard it said | There is an art which in their piedness shares | With great creating nature. (*Perdita has reservations about the artificiality of carnations*)

This is an art | Which does mend nature — change it rather — but | The art itself is nature. (*Polixenes defends the practice of grafting*)

Daffodils, | That come before the swallow dares, and take | The winds of March with beauty. (*Perdita's language invests spring flowers with courage and exhilaration*)

Nothing she does or seems | But smacks of something greater than herself, | Too noble for this place. (*Polixenes marvels at Perdita's poise*)

One being dead, | I shall have more than you can dream of yet… (*Florizel tactlessly anticipates what he will inherit on his father's death*)

I'll have thy beauty scratched with briars and made | More homely than thy state. (*Polixenes's threats to Perdita express class contempt*)

…I was about to speak and tell him plainly | The self-same sun that shines upon his court | Hides not his visage from our cottage but | Looks on alike. (*Perdita engages in social egalitarianism*)

If I might die within this hour, I have lived | To die when I desire. (*The Shepherd bemoans his fate*)

…Not for Bohemia, nor the pomp that may | Be thereat gleaned, for all the sun sees, or | The close earth wombs, or the profound seas hides | In unknown fathoms, will I break my oath | To this my fair beloved. (*Florizel expresses his constancy*)

…I think affliction may subdue the cheek, | But not take in the mind. (*Perdita asserts her moral courage*)

Ha, ha, what a fool Honesty is! And Trust, his sworn brother, a very simple gentleman! (*Autolycus cynically delights in the rewards of his trade*)

Act V scene 1

Whilst I remember | Her and her virtues, I cannot forget | My blemishes in them… (*Leontes expresses his continuing remorse*)

Stars, stars, | And all eyes else dead coals! (*Leontes remembers Hermione's eyes*)

Welcome hither, | As is the spring to th'earth! (*Leontes welcomes Florizel and Perdita as bringers of new life*)

The blessèd gods | Purge all infection from our air whilst you | Do climate here! (*Leontes wishes his visitors a healthy stay*)

Act V scene 2

Such a deal of wonder is broken out within this hour that ballad-makers cannot be able to express it. […] This news, which is called true, is so like an old tale that the verity of it is in strong suspicion. (*The 2nd Gentleman marvels at the unlikeliness of offstage events*)

But O the noble combat that 'twixt joy and sorrow was fought in Paulina! She had one eye declined for the loss of her husband, another elevated that the oracle was fulfilled. (*The 3rd Gentleman describes Paulina's mixed reaction*)

Act V scene 3

…Dear queen, that ended when I but began, | Give me that hand of yours to kiss. (*Perdita addresses her mother's statue*)

My lord, your sorrow was too sore laid on, | Which sixteen winters cannot blow away, | So many summers dry. (*Camillo gently criticises Leontes's excessive mourning*)

It is required | You do awake your faith. (*Paulina demands a renewal of Leontes's spiritual convictions*)

If this be magic, let it be an art | Lawful as eating. (*Leontes hopes Hermione's reanimation is not due to occult powers*)

You gods, look down, | And from your sacred vials pour your graces | Upon my daughter's head! (*Hermione invokes divine blessings upon her daughter*)

Selected glossary of literary terms

Note: Terms are defined here in their literary sense; they often have alternative meanings in other contexts. Cross-references to other glossary entries are printed in bold.

allegory a literary form in which the characters and events in the story represent something in a **symbolic** way and offer a moral lesson. Allegories often feature characters who are **personified** abstractions, such as Holy Church (William Langland, *Piers Plowman*) or the Giant Despair (John Bunyan, *The Pilgrim's Progress*). See also **fable**.

alliteration	the repetition of initial consonant sounds in words placed comparatively near to each other. This can be emphatic, or can enhance the effect of **onomatopocia**.
allusion	a passing reference to something — an event, person, myth, literary work, piece of music — which the writer does not explain, presumably expecting it to be within the reader's general knowledge.
ambiguous	having two or more possible interpretations, but leaving in doubt which is correct. Textual ambiguity may be deliberate or accidental.
ambivalent	having contradictory feelings or attitudes towards something; having either or both of two contrary or parallel values, qualities or meanings.
antithesis	a balancing of words or phrases of opposite meaning, e.g. 'paid down	More *penitence* than done *trespass*' (V.1.3–4).
aside	a remark spoken by a character in a play which is unheard by some or all of the other characters on stage. It may be shared directly with the audience.
assonance	identical vowel sounds in words placed comparatively near to each other in a piece of writing to create particular effects of emphasis, echo, **onomatopoeia** etc., e.g. brown/found/howl/sour.
atmosphere	the emotional **tone** conjured up by a particular use of language, the mood or feeling created.
blank verse	unrhymed **iambic pentameter**.
caesura	a mid-line break in a **verse** line, coinciding with the end of a grammatical unit, e.g. 'The sessions shall proceed: this is mere falsehood' (III.2.138).
caricature	an exaggerated, unrealistic character in fiction or drama, built around a limited number of character traits such as greed or naïvety.
characterisation	the techniques by which a writer creates fictional or dramatic characters. These might include description, authorial comment, **dialogue**, **symbolism**, interior monologue, **soliloquy** etc.
chorus	in Greek **tragedy**, a group of characters, speaking in unison, whose function was to comment on the events of the play. In Shakespeare, usually a single character, sometimes a personified abstraction like Time in *The Winter's Tale*, who combines the functions of storyteller and commentator.
climax	a moment of intensity and power to which a play or story has been leading.

colloquial	the language of speech rather than writing, informal in grammar and vocabulary, possibly using dialect or employing the phraseology of slang.
comedy	a **dramatic genre** in which events reach a positive outcome, often concluding in betrothal or marriage, or in the exposure of vice and folly. Although comedy often contains elements of humour, this is not a prerequisite of the genre.
denouement	the unfolding of the final stages of a dramatic or fictional **plot**, usually at or just after the **climax**.
dialogue	the direct speech of characters in fiction or drama engaged in conversation.
diction	a writer's choice of words. Diction may be formal, **colloquial**, poetic, **ironic**, artificial etc. It helps to create the **tone** and mood of a piece of writing, and in drama can be an instrument of **characterisation**.
dramatic	pertaining to the **genre** of drama. If you are asked to consider whether part of a play is 'dramatic', you are not being asked to say whether it is *exciting*, but whether it contributes to the overall impact of the play.
dramatic irony	a discrepancy between the perceptions of the audience and those of the characters in a play. Dramatic irony may create humour or tension.
dumb show	a dramatic interlude in which a key part of the story is presented without dialogue, using mime, action and gesture, often accompanied by music.
eclectic	drawing on a wide range of reference from diverse sources.
emotive language	language that arouses an emotional response in the reader or hearer.
end-stopped line	a line of **verse** in which the grammatical sense is completed at the end of the line, e.g. 'The bug which you would fright me with, I seek' (III.2.90). The opposite of **enjambement**.
enjamb[e]ment	running the sense from one line of verse over to the next without a pause at the end of the line, e.g. 'This your request | Is altogether just' (III.2.114–15).
epilogue	a speech that rounds off a play, either summing up its events, reflecting on its conclusion or inviting the audience's applause. It may be spoken by a character, an actor stepping out of character or a **chorus** figure.
exposition	the delivery of crucial information to the audience, usually at the start of a play, filling in the background to the characters and the **plot**.

fable	an **allegory** in which the characters are animals.
farce	a variety of dramatic **comedy** in which the humour derives mostly from complicated situations such as misunderstanding, deception and mistaken identity.
feminine ending	a light or unstressed syllable at the end of a line of **verse**, e.g. 'The Emperor of Russia was my father' (III.2.117).
First Folio	the first collected edition of Shakespeare's works, published in 1623. *The Winter's Tale* had not been printed prior to its appearance in the Folio.
genre	a classification of literary texts (or other artistic forms) according to type. *The Winter's Tale* might be classified as a **tragicomedy** or **romance**. Genre classification can be unhelpful in simplifying complex works into convenient terminology. *The Winter's Tale*, for example, also contains elements of **pastoral**.
hyperbole	exaggeration, usually for poetic or dramatic effect.
iambic pentameter	a line of **verse** consisting of five iambic feet (see **metrical foot**).
imagery	a pattern of related images that helps to build up mood and **atmosphere**, deepen our response to characters or develop the **themes** of a literary work.
incongruity	when something is or seems out of place in its context, for example a joke at the climax of a **tragedy**.
irony	a discrepancy between the actual and implied meaning of language, illustrated in its crudest verbal form by sarcasm. Irony can be complex and subtle in the hands of great writers, though it can be difficult to pick up the ironic **tone**. See also **dramatic irony**.
masque	a form of entertainment combining elaborate poetry, music and scenic spectacle, particularly popular at the courts of James I and Charles I. Dramatists of the period often introduced masque-like elements into their plays, such as the statue scene in *The Winter's Tale*.
metaphor	an imaginative identification between one thing and another, e.g. 'Stars, stars, | And all eyes else dead coals!' (V.1.67–68).
metatheatrical	a self-conscious awareness in a play of its status as a theatrical performance. Such an awareness might work through the persistent use of theatrical **metaphor**, or through more substantial devices such as a play within the play.
metre	a particular pattern of rhythmical organisation based on the number and distribution of stressed syllables in a line. There are a number of common metres in English verse, the most common being **iambic pentameter**.

metrical foot	one unit of a line of **verse**, consisting of two or three syllables with different patterns of **stress**. For example, an **iambic** foot has two syllables, the second of which is stressed. The metre is determined by the number of particular kinds of feet in a line.
morality play	a kind of religious drama popular in fifteenth- and sixteenth-century England, often in the form of **allegory**, peopled by **personified** abstractions such as Knowledge, and representative characters like Everyman.
onomatopoeia	the use of words that imitate the sounds they describe (e.g. fizz, spit, crash); or a combination of words where the sound seems to echo the sense. **Assonance** and **alliteration** can often be used to create an onomatopoeic effect.
oxymoron	a condensed **antithesis**; usually a phrase of two words, apparently opposite in meaning, which ought to cancel each other out, e.g. 'darkness visible' (John Milton, *Paradise Lost*); 'oppressive liberty' (George Eliot, *Middlemarch*).
pastoral	a literary **genre** set in an idealised, artificial and unrealistic rural landscape, with shepherds and shepherdesses as the main characters.
personification	a variety of **metaphor** which attributes human qualities to something inanimate or abstract, e.g. 'Good expedition be my friend' (I.2.458).
physical comedy	humour derived purely from stage actions such as falling over, picking pockets and throwing custard pies. Sometimes called slapstick.
plagiarism	stealing someone else's ideas and passing them off as your own; intellectual theft. Writers are often accused of this, but it was not regarded as particularly serious in Shakespeare's time, when playwrights frequently plundered the work of other writers for ideas.
plot	the organisation and structuring of the narrative and its characters in a novel or play.
prologue	a speech that precedes the main action of a play, often spoken by a **chorus** or similar character not involved in the story.
prompt-book	the annotated copy of a playscript used in managing and running a theatrical performance.
prose	the language of everyday speech and writing, distinguished from poetry or **verse**.
pun	a play on words, sometimes for humorous effect. It commonly plays on two words of similar sound but different meaning (e.g. beat/bait, II.3.91–92), or a single word containing more than one meaning (e.g. neat, I.2.123–25).

resolution	the tying up of loose ends at the end of a fictional or dramatic narrative, during or immediately after the **denouement**.
rhetoric	the art of using language to persuade. Rhetoric was taught as a subject in Elizabethan schools, modelled on classical examples, identifying a range of specific linguistic techniques which a good persuasive speaker or writer was expected to use.
rhyme	identical sounds repeated at the ends of **verse** lines in a variety of patterns. The last stressed vowel sound and everything that follows it should be identical, e.g. Time/crime, leaving/ grieving (IV.1).
rhyming couplet	a pair of adjacent **rhyming** lines.
romance	a literary and dramatic **genre** usually portraying unrealistic characters in fantastic adventures set in imaginary countries. Romances often contain elements of fairy tale, deal with the trials and tribulations of love, and end happily.
satire	a literary form in which people, institutions and aspects of human behaviour are attacked through humour, by being made to appear ridiculous.
simile	an imaginative comparison of one thing with another, drawing attention to itself by using the words *like* or *as*, e.g. 'he that wears her like her medal, hanging	About his neck' (I.2.307–08).
soliloquy	a speech in a play, usually of some length, delivered by a character alone on stage. Characters may address the audience directly, or we may feel we are sharing their thoughts. Traditionally, soliloquies were considered to reveal the genuine feelings of a character, free of equivocation and deception.
sources	the inspirations, drawn from history, mythology or other literary and dramatic works, that writers build into their own artistic vision.
stereotype	a fictional or **dramatic** character conforming to a narrow set of characteristics assumed to be typical of a particular group.
stress	the natural emphasis we put on particular syllables in words when we speak. Used to construct rhythmical patterns of **metre** when composing **verse**.
sub-plot	a subordinate storyline in a fictional or **dramatic** narrative, with its own set of characters, that works alongside or interlocks with the main **plot**.
subtext	the meaning implied by or underlying the explicit language of a text.

symbolism	the explicit or implied representation of a thing or idea by something else. A dove may symbolise peace, or a heart, love. Literary and **dramatic** symbolism may be complex, for example in Polixenes's and Perdita's discussion of flowers.
tableau	the visual arrangement of characters and objects as if in a picture.
theme	an issue or idea developed in a work of literature. Most complex texts have a variety of themes.
tone	a particular quality in the use of language that may indicate the writer's or speaker's attitude to the reader or listener, or may create a particular mood or **atmosphere**. A tone may be formal, sincere, pompous, gloomy, ironic, solemn, cheerful etc.
tragedy	a **dramatic genre** focusing on the downfall or death of one or two central characters, usually of elevated social status.
tragicomedy	a **dramatic genre** mingling elements of **tragedy** and **comedy** and normally arriving at a happy ending. The contrasting elements may be in separate sections, as in *The Winter's Tale*, or mingled together through the play, as in *Cymbeline*.
unities	'rules of drama', originally propounded by Aristotle in the fourth century BC, that the action of a play should be more or less continuous, enacted in one location and taking place within a 24-hour period. Called the unities of time, place and action, these classical notions were frequently flouted in Elizabethan and Jacobean drama, though seventeenth-century French drama placed great importance on them. Shakespeare ignores the unities completely in *The Winter's Tale*.
verse	language organised according to its rhythmical qualities into regular patterns of metre. Verse may or may not **rhyme**, but is usually set out in lines.

Questions & Answers

LITERATURE

Essay questions, specimen plans and notes

Coursework essays

In choosing a coursework essay, you must always check with your teacher that it fits the requirements of the course you are following. For example, it would be foolish to choose a title that focuses on Assessment Objectives that are not covered in the coursework part of your specification.

You may have valid ideas of your own for an essay title or subject. Again, these should be discussed with your teacher. Make sure you know the number of words you are allowed for the essay.

Suggested titles

1 What kind of a play is *The Winter's Tale*? How successfully do you think it works as a text for the theatre?

Here are some ideas for tackling this essay:

- discussion of the genres of tragicomedy, romance and pastoral in the context of Jacobean theatre
- exploitation of indoor facilities of Blackfriars Theatre, while remaining appropriate for outdoor performance at the Globe
- analysis of overall structure of the play: tragedy, comedy, resolution; the two worlds of Sicilia and Bohemia
- some comment on principal themes of the play and the imagery that supports them, relating this to both structure and genre
- relevance of the play's portrayal of monarchy and rural life to contemporary social and political ideas, e.g. the issue of succession; women's place in society; the relative merits of court and country, art and nature; social divisions; attitudes to rogues and vagabonds
- the kind of characters in the play, the dramatic effectiveness of the characterisation and the possibilities for actors to realise the characters in performance
- dramatic qualities of the play, especially the use of contrast between high drama, low comedy, idealised romance, spectacular moments, music and song, masque-like elements, verse and prose etc.
- effect on the audience, e.g. how dramatic, funny, moving the play is; which parts work best, which are less successful: consider how you think the members of the audience should feel as they leave a good production of the play

2 What contrasts are drawn in the text between the worlds of Sicilia and Bohemia? How might these contrasts be represented on stage?

3 What elements of realism do you find in the characters and social worlds of the play?

4 Explore the character of Leontes, showing how he develops through the play and saying how convincing you find him.

5 Choose any two characters who offer interesting points for comparison and contrast. Write an essay comparing their characters and roles in the play, saying what you think of them. (Suggestions: Camillo and Antigonus; Hermione and Paulina; Autolycus and the Shepherd; Leontes and Polixenes; Florizel and the Clown; Hermione and Perdita.)

6 What is the function of Autolycus in the play, and how successfully does he fulfil it?

7 How does Shakespeare portray the women in the play? Examine the characterisation and role of the female characters.

8 Does Shakespeare succeed in individualising the minor characters so as to make them interesting parts to act as well as contributing to the dramatic effects of the play? Consider four or five examples to support your answer. (Suggestions: Archidamus; Cleomenes and Dion; Emilia; Mamillius; Mopsa and Dorcas; the Shepherd's servant; the three Gentlemen.)

9 Write about the different kinds of humour and comedy in the play.

10 Write about some of the themes you consider to be important in the play and show how they are developed.

11 Write about the imagery of the play and the effects it creates.

12 Choose one scene, or a self-contained segment within a scene, and give a full analysis of it, commenting on what it reveals of characters and themes; its dramatic effect; its supporting imagery; and anything else that interests you.

13 Choose one scene and describe how you would present it on stage. (You will need to give some preliminary account of the type of theatre you envisage as well as the overall production style.)

14 Imagine you are a director who wishes to stage a production of *The Winter's Tale*. Explain in a preliminary note what kind of theatre and company you work for (large or small; amateur or professional; rich or poor; commercial or subsidised; indoor or open-air; traditional or experimental; touring or home-based). Then write a letter to your artistic director or board outlining your reasons for considering this a good play to stage, and giving an outline of your approach to the production.

15 How useful have you found it to study the play in the context of Shakespeare and his time?

16 How has your understanding of the play been enhanced by your reading of a variety of literary criticism? What critical views have you encountered that you consider particularly interesting, revealing or controversial?

17 Write a comparison of *The Winter's Tale*, or any appropriate aspect of it, with

another Shakespeare play that you know well. (*As You Like It*, *Much Ado about Nothing*, *Othello*, *Pericles*, *Cymbeline* or *The Tempest* would be good choices.)

18 Write a review of any production of the play you have seen — on stage, film or television. You should comment on the interpretation of the play and the characters; the sets, costumes, music, lighting, performances; and anything else you consider important. If you are lucky enough to have seen more than one production, you could write a comparison.

Tackling production-related questions

There can be no substitute for seeing a play in performance — preferably on stage. There is an electricity about live performance, a sense of danger and risk as well as of shared experience, that cannot be captured on film or television. Your response to a production will be as personal and subjective as that to any other cultural experience. You should, however, make some attempt to understand what it is trying to achieve, and judge it accordingly.

The Winter's Tale is a brilliant performance piece, but you should be prepared for disappointments. It is an extremely difficult play to bring off successfully, and productions often fail to bring the Bohemian scenes to life.

The impact of a production may depend on the kind of theatre in which it is staged. A small, intimate theatre, with the audience on three or four sides, can offer a kind of psychologically intense and detailed performance that may be more difficult to achieve in a large theatre with a proscenium stage. A large theatre, though, has more scope for spectacular presentation.

Clues to a production's approach and emphasis can often be found in publicity materials such as brochures and posters, and in the programme. These are always worth a look, both before and after you see the show.

- What signals do they give about the play itself and the approach taken to it in the production?

Theatres today rarely have stage curtains which are closed before the performance.

- What clues were there to the production style in what you saw as you took your place in the theatre before the play started?

The opening moments of a production signal its style, too. It is quite rare for *The Winter's Tale* to begin exactly as it does in the text, with a bare stage, the entry of Camillo and Archidamus, and their spoken dialogue.

- How did the production begin? Was there music, a visual display or dumb show, the swift creation of a stage setting, or anything else not specified in the text?
- What was the intention behind such an opening, and how effective was it?

When reflecting on a production, there are various aspects to consider. These are discussed below.

The world of the play

- What was the overall setting of the play? Was it performed in the period in which the story is set, the period in which the play was written, in a modern setting, or some other period? Perhaps there was a more eclectic approach, with elements from a variety of periods and cultures?
- Why do you think this decision had been made? Did it work? In particular, if a modern setting was chosen, did you find it helped you to understand the social and political aspects of the play, or was it jarring to see the characters using guns, mobile phones and laptops while speaking of daggers, letters and the gods?
- There are two contrasting worlds in *The Winter's Tale*. How were they represented visually? Was much scenery or furniture used? Did this change between scenes? Was there any use of backdrops or projections? What kind of colour schemes were employed? How were lighting, music and sound effects used to enhance the mood and atmosphere of the settings? Was Sicilia in Act V different from Sicilia in Acts I–III?
- How were the characters costumed? Did their costumes suggest appropriate ideas about their personality, social status and dramatic role? What costume changes did characters have?
- Were there any particularly striking effects? How were key moments staged — the trial, the bear, the sheep-shearing and the statue?

The use of the text

- Were you aware of any cuts, alterations, additions or transpositions? Why do you think such textual changes were made?
- Were any characters doubled? Was this merely due to expediency, or did it make a particular point?
- Where did any intervals come in the play? Were they at appropriate moments or did they break the dramatic continuity?
- Was the text spoken well? Was the story told clearly? Was any special emphasis given to particular words, lines or speeches?
- Was the performance paced effectively?

The performances

In responding to actors' performances, it is particularly important to recognise the difference between a bad performance and a performance that differs from your own understanding of a role. A bad performance might be technically inadequate — inaudible, lacking in energy and charisma, delivering lines without apparently understanding their meaning etc. An interpretation of a role may be misguided or perverse but performed brilliantly, and should cause you to reassess your own interpretation.

- Which performances were most powerful and effective? What made them so?
- Were you surprised by any of the actors' interpretations?

- Did any roles come to life in performance in a way that they didn't when you were studying the text?
- Did the actors work well together as an ensemble?

Your overall response

- Did the production work well for you as a theatrical entertainment? Were you engrossed, amused, moved or bored? How can you explain these responses?
- Did the production do justice to the play? Did it change your view of the play?

Theatre is a collaborative activity, and in writing about a production you need to show some awareness of the roles of the various practitioners. Those in the front line are obviously the actors, but their performances will have been shaped by the director, who is also responsible for the overall concept and interpretation. Much of what you remember from a production, though, may well be the contribution of the designer, while the practicalities of the smooth running of each performance are the responsibility of the stage manager. Other roles, such as those of lighting designer, sound designer, composer and music director speak for themselves.

Exam essays

You can use the questions below as the basis of your own exam practice: to refine your brainstorming and planning skills, or to tackle a complete essay in the appropriate time limit. Choose the type of question that is relevant for the specification you are following; in AQA (A), for example, the questions normally ask you to respond to two contrasting critical viewpoints on the play. Remember to refer to the *play* and the *audience*, not the *book* and the *reader*. Remain imaginatively aware of the play's *performance* potential.

Whole text questions

Questions 8, 9, 22, 24, 25, 26, 28, 35, 37, 40, 42, 43, 45 are more suitable for open book exams.

Genre and context

1 **What do you understand by the terms tragicomedy and romance? How useful do you think it is to consider *The Winter's Tale* as an example of these dramatic genres?**

2 **How far do you think the play's title reflects its genre?**

3 ***The Winter's Tale* was probably performed by the King's Men at both the open-air Globe and the indoor Blackfriars theatres. How might the experience of seeing the play have been different at these two venues?**

4 **What elements of social and political awareness have you found in *The Winter's Tale*?**

5 How far does *The Winter's Tale* reflect Jacobean views on *two* of the following: friendship; marriage; women in society?

6 What are some of the reservations that previous critics have expressed about *The Winter's Tale*, and how would you respond to them?

7 Outline four or five specific ways in which a modern production of *The Winter's Tale* might be different from a Jacobean staging, and comment on how these might influence an audience's response to the play.

Characters

8 How does Shakespeare present the onset of Leontes's jealousy in Act I scene 2?

9 Compare the portrayal of Leontes in Act V with his presentation in Acts I–III. By what means does Shakespeare suggest the changes in his character?

10 Write about the development of Hermione's character throughout the play.

11 Analyse Paulina's role in *The Winter's Tale*, paying particular attention to her dramatic effectiveness.

12 Is Polixenes merely a necessary instrument of the plot, or do you think Shakespeare makes him an interesting character in his own right?

13 Some modern productions have doubled the roles of Hermione and Perdita. What is there in the play to justify such a decision, and what technical difficulties does it create?

14 How do you respond to Camillo and Antigonus as examples of loyal service to their royal masters?

15 Are Florizel and Perdita any more than idealised romantic lovers?

16 What inconsistencies are there in Shakespeare's portrayal of the Shepherd, and how do you account for them?

17 What kind of laughter is evoked by the Clown's role in the play?

18 Autolycus is almost entirely dispensable from the play's plot. Why do you think he is in *The Winter's Tale*?

19 Choose one of the principal roles in the play. As a director, what advice would you give at the start of rehearsals to the actor playing this role?

20 How effectively does Shakespeare present the minor characters? Write about three or four such characters whose roles you consider to be significant.

21 How dramatically fitting is the proposed marriage between Paulina and Camillo at the end of the play?

22 What features are there in the speech of Time that suggest how his character might have been portrayed on stage?

Setting and atmosphere

23 How would you describe the mood and atmosphere associated with *either* Leontes's jealousy *or* the sheep-shearing festivities? How is this atmosphere created?

24 Consider *either* the scene in which Cleomenes and Dion describe Apollo's oracle (III.1), *or* the scene of Perdita's exposure (III.3.1–57). How does Shakespeare create the atmosphere of the scene through its language?

25 Contrast the atmosphere of Leontes's court in Acts I–III with that in Act V.

26 How would you create the atmosphere of any one scene of the play in a modern stage production? Consider the use of set, costumes, lighting, music, movement and sound effects, and explain how these would support specific features of the text.

Themes

27 What do you think the play has to say about jealousy and its effects?

28 What is the relevance of Polixenes and Perdita's discussion of grafting to the play as a whole?

29 What kind of religious ideas does the play evoke for you?

30 Shakespeare's main source, Greene's *Pandosto*, is subtitled *The Triumph of Time*. How appropriate would this be as a subtitle for *The Winter's Tale*?

31 What kinds of deception are portrayed in *The Winter's Tale*? What are the different motives for such deception, and what effects do they have?

32 Examine *two* of the principal relationships in the play and consider what they reveal about love, friendship, marriage, parenthood or loyalty.

33 What do you consider to be the central theme of the play, and how is it developed?

Structure and dramatic effect

34 Write an account of the play's overall structure, considering how it supports the play's narrative, themes and dramatic impact.

35 Write an analysis of how Shakespeare manipulates dramatic tension in *either* the trial scene (III.2), *or* the statue scene (V.3).

36 What kinds of humour are developed in Acts I–III of the play?

37 Do you consider *'Exit, pursued by a bear'* to be a dramatic or a comic moment? Justify your answer in terms of the overall structure of the play.

38 What is the function of song, dance and spectacular effects in the play?

39 Time asks us to 'Impute it not a crime' that he passes over 16 years at the start of Act IV. How would you defend Shakespeare's disregard of the unities in *The Winter's Tale*?

40 Examine closely the dramatic structure of one of the five acts of the play.

Language

41 What are some of the recurring images that Shakespeare uses in the play, and what effect does such imagery have?

42 Examine two or three of the prose sections in the play. Consider aspects of Shakespeare's prose style, suggest why these sections are in prose and not verse, and assess their impact in the dramatic context.

43 The verse of Shakespeare's last plays has been noted for its metrical irregularity, its fractured grammar and tortured syntax. Choose a verse speech from *The Winter's Tale* and show how it either conforms to or contrasts with such characteristics.

Contrasting critical viewpoints

44 'Camillo is an old rogue whom I can hardly forgive for his double treachery' (Hartley Coleridge, 1851). 'Camillo is [...] one of the touchstones of decency and sanity against which the audience can measure the behaviour of other characters in the play [...], the latest in a long line of selfless, fiercely loyal servants to Shakespearean kings' (Lynn and Jeff Wood, 1999). Which of these views of Camillo do you think best reflects the character Shakespeare has created?

45 Act V scene 2 has aroused differing opinions. Mark van Doren was disappointed that 'the recognition of Leontes and his daughter takes place off stage; we only hear three gentlemen talking prose about it' (1939), and Sir Arthur Quiller-Couch called it 'the greatest fault of all' in the play (1915). Nevill Coghill, conversely, judged the scene 'among the most gripping and memorable of the entire play', adding that Shakespeare 'decided on a messenger-speech scene for several voices (an unusual experiment) and made a masterpiece of it' (1958). What are your views on the Gentlemen's conversation in this scene?

46 S. L. Bethell commented in 1947 that the play's 'stagecraft [might be] justifiably described as crude or naïve'. Nevill Coghill responded in 1958 by asserting that 'Shakespeare's stagecraft in this play is [...] novel, subtle and revolutionary'. Consider these two views and offer your own assessment of Shakespeare's stagecraft in *The Winter's Tale*.

47 'Spring breaks through the grip of winter, love returns, enabling Leontes to awake his faith and be redeemed' (Trevor Nunn, theatre director, 1969). 'Trevor Nunn pompously interprets this popular nonsense as some profound allegory about a search for love through suffering and ultimate redemption' (Milton Shulman, theatre reviewer, 1969). Popular nonsense or profound allegory: what do *you* think of *The Winter's Tale*?

Passage-based questions

When tackling passage-based analysis, depending on the precise nature of the question, you should consider the points outlined below:

- Is the section in prose, verse or a mixture of the two? What is notable about the way these language modes are used?
- What is its place in the development of the plot?
- What is going on between the characters present, and what is the impact of any entrances and exits?
- What is the impact of characters who say little in the section?

- How does the language of the scene reveal character?
- What is the balance between dialogue and soliloquy, longer and shorter speeches?
- How does the section support the wider imagery and themes of the play?
- How is the stage picture, together with action and movement, suggested through the dialogue and any stage directions?
- Are there any levels of irony or dramatic irony in the sequence?
- Which characters engage the audience's sympathy, and why?
- What is the function of the set section in the dramatic structure of the play? Are there any parallels or contrasts with other episodes? What would the play lose without this section?

1 Write an analysis of Act I scene 1. How effectively does it begin the play?

2 Reread Act I scene 2 lines 1–108. What impression of Hermione is created in this section?

3 Look again at Leontes's speeches at Act I scene 2 lines 108–20, 128–46 and 179–207. How does Shakespeare create his state of mind in these speeches?

4 Examine the dramatic impact of Act II scene 1 lines 1–32. Why is this section important in terms of what follows in the remainder of the scene?

5 Compare the impact made on their first appearances by Antigonus (II.1.126–99) and Paulina (II.2.1–66).

6 Reread Act II scene 3 lines 26–129. Analyse the scope for humour that Shakespeare builds into this sequence.

7 What is the function of Cleomenes and Dion in Act III scene 1 and Act V scene 1 lines 1–84? How important is it that the same two characters are involved in these scenes?

8 Look carefully at Hermione's speeches in the trial scene (III.2.20–121). How is she different from the Hermione of Act I scene 2 lines 1–108?

9 Write a full analysis of Paulina's speech beginning, 'What studied torments, tyrant, hast for me?' (III.2.172–99).

10 Assess the impact of the first part of Act III scene 3, lines 1–57, paying particular attention to its position in the play.

11 How does Shakespeare change the mood and tone of the play in the second half of Act III scene 3, lines 58–119?

12 Time's speech (Act IV scene 1) has been accused of being clumsy and old-fashioned, with jingling rhymes. How valid is this criticism? Offer a critical analysis of the speech as part of your response.

13 What are some of the main features of Act IV scene 2? How does it act as a structural parallel to Act I scene 1?

14 Look again at Autolycus's songs (IV.3, IV.4.211–305). Write a commentary on the songs, showing how they reflect both Autolycus's character and the wider concerns of the play.

15 How does Shakespeare present the Clown in Act IV scene 3? Is he consistent with the younger version of himself introduced at the end of Act III?

16 Write a close analysis of Florizel and Perdita's verse at the start of Act IV scene 4, lines 1–54. How is the language instrumental in creating our first impressions of the young lovers?

17 Reread Act IV scene 4 lines 70–135. What impression of Perdita is created in her flower speeches?

18 Reread Act IV scene 4 lines 322–420. How do you respond to Polixenes and Florizel in this sequence?

19 Look at Autolycus's three solo speeches in Act IV scene 4 (lines 574–92, 639–51, 772–80). How do these speeches develop his character and his relationship with the audience?

20 Write a comparison of the two comic encounters Autolycus has with the Shepherd and Clown (IV.4.652–71, V.2.99–142).

21 Look again at the first part of Act V scene 1, as far as the entrance of the servant at line 84. How would you describe the atmosphere of this section, and how is it supported by the imagery?

22 Reread the servant's speeches announcing the arrival of Florizel and his princess (V.1.85–114). How is the servant characterised? How does he compare with the Shepherd's servant in Act IV scene 4 lines 181–207, 306–21?

23 What impression do Florizel and Perdita create on their arrival in Leontes's court (V.1.114–232)?

24 Write an analysis of the Gentlemen's language in Act V scene 2 lines 1–89. What effect does it have on you?

25 Write an account of Paulina's stage-management of the statue episode in Act V scene 3.

26 How appropriate and effective do you find Act V scene 3 as a conclusion to the play?

Essay plans

1 'It has all the licence and all the charm of a fairy tale' (Arthur Symons, 1890). 'The play is about the process of social change in seventeenth-century England' (Charles Barber, 1964). What do you think each of these critics has in mind in their comments on *The Winter's Tale*, and do you think their critical views are mutually exclusive?

Possible ideas to include in a plan

Introduction

- at face value, the play's title suggests its status as fairy tale – something entertaining, not necessarily to be taken seriously
- does this preclude the play from also dealing with more serious issues?

Fairy-tale elements

- examine Symons's terminology: 'licence' suggests anything can happen – spontaneous jealousy, oracles, bears, rescued babies, statues coming to life
- 'charm' is a more difficult term to define: perhaps applies more to the pastoral scenes and romantic lovers
- fairy tales contain strong elements of danger and evil, with virtue and happiness threatened – relate to plot of play
- fairy tales generally have positive outcomes, often with a sense of magic – relate to ending of play
- Shakespeare himself draws attention to his play as a 'tale' – see II.1.22–31; V.2.23, 49; V.3.115–17; plus Autolycus's ballads, IV.4.245–68

Social change

- various elements possibly considered by Barber
- court and country; art and nature – could be considered social issues: see 'flower debate', Perdita's remarks on social equality (IV.4.421–25), Perdita's status as princess raised by shepherds
- Shepherd's social rise, first through discovery of money ('Let my sheep go', III.3.110), then through royal patronage – consider imported products they are able to buy for sheep-shearing
- Autolycus's status as former courtier, now 'masterless man' – a social threat

Conclusion

- discuss which of these elements of the play are likely to be most obvious to an audience
- fairy-tale elements are inescapable, but the play's social concerns seem incidental to its overall effect – they are not, though, mutually exclusive

Top band marking guidelines

Note: Not all AOs carry equal weight in all specifications.

AO1 Coherent and lucid expression in a relevant and well-organised answer. A clear conceptual grasp of the meaning of fairy tale and social relevance. A sense of balance between the two views expressed, and a clearly argued weighing-up of their relative significance.

AO2 Evidence of detailed knowledge and accurate understanding of text. Confident grasp of how texts may be multi-layered and work simultaneously in different modes. Ability to summon supporting evidence/quotations. Shows skill and ease in ranging through play to construct argument.

AO3 Demonstrates awareness of how play's form, structure and language create its fairy-tale qualities, and how language, character and action promote social ideas. Quotations skilfully unpacked to elucidate significance.

AO4 Confidence in offering independent judgements on issues raised, and in handling alternative viewpoints without being intimidated by the status of literary critics. Opinions are conceptualised and effectively argued. Possible reference to critics other than those quoted in question.

AO5 Shows grasp of sociopolitical context of play, including genre issues and the sense that Jacobean drama engages with contemporary cultural debates. Sense of *audience*, not *readers*, as key receptors of dramatic text, and judging potential audience awareness of differing textual elements.

2 Do you think *The Winter's Tale* offers a stereotypical view of women, or does it challenge women's traditional role in society?

Possible ideas to include in a plan

Introduction

- views of Shakespeare's female characters have changed from century to century as women's social status has changed
- Victorian critics, for example, tended to idealise Hermione, Paulina and Perdita as emblems of noble and selfless womanhood: courageous, dignified, patient, loyal and forgiving
- in our century we can be aware of elements of female stereotypes in the characters, but also see them as a critique of such stereotyping

Stereotypes

- the three central women fall into particular stereotypes: the nagging scold, the victimised wife, the beautiful princess
- Mopsa and Dorcas are also stereotyped as jealous rivals
- Paulina especially is defined by Leontes as shrewish wife and even witch (see II.3)
- Shakespeare allows the women themselves to refer to anti-feminist stereotypes – see II.1.108–09, III.2.217–18, V.3.89–91
- Perdita's association with flowers seems to make her an emblem of fragile beauty
- other women are either impotent victims of patriarchal power (Hermione's ladies, Antigonus's daughters) or models of domesticity (Shepherd's wife)
- all the play's major actions are initiated by men; the women merely respond

Stereotypes challenged

- despite the above, it is the women of the play who are the characters we admire – in varying degrees they stand up against male tyranny
- they are not idealised, however, but given human weaknesses and errors of judgement: Hermione fails to read Leontes's state of mind, Paulina leaves the baby unprotected

- Perdita's flower speeches could be interpreted as suggestive of strength, e.g. the power and vigour of the daffodils
- the play's regenerative outcome is entirely due to female power and management of events

Performance issues

- our views of women's roles can be strongly affected by staging
- status of women inevitably diminished by original performance by boy actors
- modern performance can enhance stronger interpretation of women's roles and role of women, e.g. staging the ending: why doesn't Hermione speak to Leontes? how does Paulina respond to being paired off with Camillo? who leads the exit and who exits with whom?

Conclusion

- Shakespeare means what he means to us *now* – we cannot recapture his 'intentions', only interpret the texts he left
- text of *The Winter's Tale* gives ample scope for seeing its women as subversive of stereotypes imposed on them by patriarchal society
- perhaps end with final image of 2001 National Theatre production: Hermione clinging to Perdita, not exiting with Leontes

Top band marking guidelines

Note: Not all AOs carry equal weight in all specifications.

AO1 Coherent and lucid expression in a relevant and well-organised answer. A clear conceptual grasp of female stereotypes and how they might be challenged. A sense of balance between the two sides of the argument.

AO2 Evidence of detailed knowledge and accurate understanding of text. Confident awareness of different ways of interpreting text. Secure grasp of roles of female characters. Shows skill and ease in ranging through play to summon supporting evidence/quotations and construct argument.

AO3 Demonstrates implicit/explicit grasp of how female characters fit into overall structure of play. Analyses how use of language both creates and overturns stereotypes. Skilfully unpacks quoted lines to explore meaning and implications.

AO4 Sense of independent analysis, but supported by occasional reference to other critical viewpoints; aware of an interpretative tradition relating to the female characters. Shows awareness of how performance can redirect response.

AO5 Awareness of cultural/sociopolitical context relating to attitudes to women in Jacobean and modern times. Shows some grasp of critical theory – avoidance of making assumptions about Shakespeare's intentions. Understands that *audience*, not *readers*, are key receptors of dramatic text, and appreciates how productions can manipulate audience response.

Specimen essays

The three essays that follow are intended to offer a sense of how different types of question might be tackled. In an exam situation, they would be structured less confidently and written less accurately, with a narrower range of direct quotation, depending on whether the text of the play was available in the exam. The same questions could be answered in a variety of different ways, with considerable change of focus and emphasis from individual candidates. Your own knowledge and understanding of the play and its contexts should give you the confidence to write effective essays on any subject the examiners can devise.

Sample essay 1

Write about some of the imagery that Shakespeare uses in *The Winter's Tale*, and its effects.

Shakespeare uses a web of interconnected patterns of imagery to achieve a variety of effects. Such imagery can create atmosphere, deepen characterisation and highlight the themes of the play.

The atmosphere associated with Leontes's court in Acts I–III is partly created through images of sickness and disease. In the first shock of his jealous rage, Leontes says he has 'tremor cordis', later talks about 'the infection of [his] brains', and comments that 'Many thousand on's | Have the disease' but 'Physic for't there's none'. From his viewpoint, the disease is Hermione's and Polixenes's imagined adultery, and he is unaware that it is, rather, his jealousy which is beginning to infect the court. Other characters seem to 'catch' the imagery of disease, such as Camillo, who talks of 'a fear | Which oft infects the wisest', but who also recognises the true source of the sickness, urging Leontes to 'be cured | Of this diseased opinion'. Leontes is not to be shaken in his belief, however, still claiming that 'were my wife's liver | Infected as her life, she would not live | The running of one glass'. It is only natural that Camillo should explain Leontes's suspicions to Polixenes in the same terms:

> There is a sickness
> Which puts some of us in distemper, but
> I cannot name the disease, and it is caught
> Of you, that yet are well.

When Polixenes realises the truth, his reaction is linguistically appropriate: 'O then my best blood turn | To an infected jelly'. From this point, the metaphorical sickness is made manifest in outbreaks of genuine physical illness, from Leontes's sleeplessness to Mamillius's 'sickness' as a result of which he 'declined, drooped, […] languished'. Ironically Mamillius, who Camillo claims 'physics the subject' – a power supposedly shared with the young Florizel who, according to Polixenes, 'with his varying childness cures in me | Thoughts that would thick my blood' – has no such curative power on his father and dies of his illness.

There is a potential cure, however. It begins its work through Paulina, who comes, she says, 'with words as med'cinal as true', and continues its power through the oracle of Apollo, whose influence on the imagery of the play in Act III scene 1 spreads a powerful antidote to the infection of the court. In just 22 lines, Cleomenes and Dion use vocabulary such as 'delicate', 'sweet', 'fertile', 'praise', 'celestial', 'reverence', 'ceremonious', 'rare', 'pleasant', 'divine' and 'gracious' to cut through the pervading atmosphere and signal an end to the disease of Leontes's jealousy.

The cure cannot be completed, though, without the influence of another contrasting world, that of the pastoral life of Bohemia. Its symbolic significance is signalled in the words of Autolycus's opening song: 'When daffodils begin to peer | [...] | The red blood reigns in the winter's pale', and its characteristic imagery is of spring and summer, birds and flowers, the last associated in particular with Perdita.

In her role as 'Mistress o'th'Feast', Perdita distributes seven different varieties of flower to the older members of the company, laments her lack of a further six that would be appropriate to her younger companions, and rejects 'carnations and streaked gillyvors' as artificial products of Man's interference with Nature. These associations could make Perdita seem like a naïve, romantic idealist, but the language in which she describes the flowers actually conveys a strong femininity reminiscent of her mother. For example, her description of daffodils presents these traditional spring flowers as both courageous, since they 'come before the swallow dares' – the strength of the image emphasised by the hard alliteration of 'daffodils [...] dares'; and powerful, since they 'take | The winds of March with beauty'. Although the primary meaning of 'take' here is to delight or enchant, we may also think of its other meanings: to seize or grab, to take control of, to take sexually, to experience and enjoy. These subtle but evocative layers of meaning attach themselves by implication to the speaker as much as to what she is speaking of, imbuing Perdita with something more than merely the freshness and beauty of the flowers she describes.

As the plot begins to resolve itself and the play's two worlds come together, so we often find opposing images quoted in parallel. Indeed, the first two speeches of Act V set up a series of suggestive antitheses. Cleomenes balances 'fault', 'trespass' and 'evil' against 'redeemed', 'penitence' and 'saint-like', while Leontes sets 'blemishes' against 'virtues', both of them converting the images of disease and cure into a more specifically religious sense. Leontes welcomes Perdita and Florizel to his court 'As is the spring to th'earth' and prays the gods to 'Purge all infection from our air whilst you | Do climate here'. His 'sin' is now outweighed in his vocabulary by words such as 'blessed', 'holy', 'graceful', 'sacred', 'worthy' and 'goodly'. In a particularly striking balance of key images, Camillo comments that Leontes's sorrow 'was too sore laid on, | Which sixteen winters cannot blow away, | So many summers dry'. And in a final reconciliation of opposing images, Art becomes Nature as Hermione's 'statue' comes to life and the play's characters, too, are reconciled.

In these examples, then, it can be seen how Shakespeare uses the imagery of disease to create the atmosphere of Leontes's court, the language of flowers to deepen our appreciation of Perdita's character, and the balancing of contrasting images to help evoke the thematic outcome of the play.

Sample essay 2

Write an analysis of the Shepherd's speech, III.3.58–73, beginning 'I would there were no age between ten and three-and-twenty'.

The arrival of the Shepherd in the play, at the height of the storm and just as Antigonus has been chased off stage by the bear, might at first seem to be something of an anticlimax. The homely language of his speech certainly supports this impression, in contrast to the formal but highly dramatic blank verse of Antigonus which precedes it. Anticlimax or not, what is certain is that the gentle comedy of the Shepherd's colloquial prose rhythms, rustic dialect and everyday concerns moves the play on to a different plane. The only link with the preceding drama is in the form of the baby Perdita, and it is her visible presence on stage that maintains the dramatic tension as the audience anticipates what the Shepherd's reaction will be when he notices her.

The Shepherd is at first preoccupied with finding two of his 'best sheep' which have been frightened off by a group of young huntsmen, leading him to reflect bitterly on the follies of youth. This opposition between youth and age, expressed here in comic form, is central to the concerns of the play and it is notable that, despite the Shepherd's strictures, it is the spirit of the young that eventually represents the play's redeeming life-force. The Shepherd identifies a somewhat extended version of adolescence, stretching from ten to twenty-three, as the troublesome age, though presumably not all the activities he complains of, such as 'getting wenches with child, wronging the ancientry, stealing, fighting', would be practised throughout that age range. His comments seem to be directed specifically at boys, which implies something about the social and domestic expectations of girls at the time, and he reserves particular venom for the wonderfully alliterative 'boiled-brains' of twenty-two year olds who are mad enough to hunt in such appalling weather. The colloquial vigour of his speech suggests a genuine anger rather than merely a stereotypical old man's comically envious criticism of the young; after all, the Shepherd's livelihood is threatened by the potential loss of his prize sheep, which are in real danger of falling prey to 'the wolf', as Antigonus did to the bear. The actor should perhaps play for genuine feeling here, rather than comic caricature.

As soon as he notices the baby, perhaps crossing himself on 'Good luck, an't be thy will', a different tone enters his speech, a tone of tenderness towards the child, succeeded by one of knowing cynicism about the ways of the world as he reflects on its likely origin. The repetitions as he takes in what he sees – 'a barne! A very pretty barne. […] A pretty one, a very pretty one' – presumably accompany a physical investigation of what he has found, as he bends down and examines it more closely. The cynicism and the tenderness come together as the Shepherd reflects that 'They were warmer that got this than the poor thing is here', but his resolution to 'take it up for pity' is checked

by an equally human nervousness as he decides to wait for the arrival of his son before he does anything else.

Throughout the speech, Shakespeare gives to the Shepherd an appropriately colloquial tone, including exclamatory phrases such as 'Hark you now', 'Good luck, an't be thy will' and 'Mercy on's'; and occasional dialect words such as 'barne', and 'child' in the sense of a girl. An actor will presumably decide to employ a regional accent to emphasise these elements; the particular accent chosen does not really matter as long as it is suggestive of a rural rather than an urban context.

Despite these features, the Shepherd's language, like that of all Shakespeare's characters, is articulate and artificially structured, with carefully crafted sentences and rhetorical patterns, such as the antithetical balance of 'which I fear the wolf will sooner find than the master', or the wry irony of 'Though I am not bookish, yet I can read'; and the grouping of three metaphorical euphemisms to explain the child's conception: 'some stair-work, some trunk-work, some behind-door-work'. The linguistic artificiality of these structures partly reminds us that characters in a play are not real people engaging in natu-ralistic discourse, but it also dignifies the Shepherd with a degree of articulate intelligence which is later enhanced by his speaking in verse in the sheep-shearing sequence.

Technically, the Shepherd's speech is a soliloquy, but clearly not one in which the character reflects internally on his deepest personal anxieties. The actor will probably decide it is best delivered direct to the audience. Although there is nothing in the speech that explicitly demands this, other than the exclamation 'Hark you now', its whole structure is suggestive of the kind of rapport with the audience – sharing with them his observations on the young, showing them the baby – that is developed much more fully in the character of Autolycus. Whatever else it does, the speech shifts us into a new dramatic world – pastoral rather than courtly, comic rather than tragic, prosaic rather than poetic. It is a real turning point.

Sample essay 3

Compare and contrast two speeches of Leontes: 'Ha'not you seen, Camillo' (I.2.267–78) and 'The blessèd gods' (V.1.167–77).

In these two speeches of more-or-less equal length, we encounter Leontes at the height of his jealousy and in the full maturity of his repentance. As befits his status, both speeches are in blank verse, but in every other respect they are strikingly dissimilar. Shakespeare employs all the subtle effects of grammar and syntax, rhythm and metre, vocabulary and image, to emphasise just how much Leontes has changed between the beginning and end of the play.

On the face of it, the metre of his speech to Camillo, in which he makes explicit the suspicions he has conceived of Hermione, seems regular. Only two lines (270 and 271) have an extra eleventh syllable, and the stresses fall more or less where the iambic beat demands. However, the grammatical patterns and syntactical structures of the speech cut across the verse rhythms, frequently obscuring the line endings with enjambements, such as 'your eye-glass | Is thicker', 'rumour | Cannot be mute', 'cogitation | Resides not', and often reaching a conclusion of the sense in strong mid-line caesuras. Just as Leontes is at odds with himself and his world, so the controlling imperatives of his language, its verse form and its grammar, are in conflict.

His Act V speech, in contrast, has only two run-on lines at the start, and its three caesuras lack the sense of strong mid-line fracture that gives such a jerky, forceful impact to his previous jealous utterances. Addressing Florizel, he is calm, reflective, regretful and gracious, and the metre suggests this as surely as it had earlier evoked his internal torment, his sarcastic and accusatory tone and his fevered jealousy.

The first speech consists essentially of only two sentences, moving through the grammatical modes of question, conditional and imperative. The question simply demands how Camillo can fail to have 'seen […] or heard […] or thought' that Hermione is 'slippery'. Each verb, however, is qualified by an elaborate parenthetical statement sarcastically suggesting that Camillo is only pretending to be ignorant of Hermione's infamy. Though the sentence is perfectly constructed, it nevertheless creates the effect of a mind constantly striking out in new directions, and it needs careful phrasing by the actor to make its meanings clear to an audience and build up to its climactic accusation. The second sentence, beginning 'If thou wilt confess', is neither grammatically clear nor logically argued, though its general drift is plain. Its awkwardness suggests an increasing lack of clarity in Leontes's own thoughts, as his emotion overwhelms his lucidity.

The speech in Act V, however, builds clearly step by step from its opening invocation of a blessing from the gods on Florizel and Perdita. In four clear statements, Leontes acknowledges how he has wronged Polixenes; accepts the punishment of his own childlessness; comments on Polixenes's good fortune in having such a worthy son; and reflects sadly on how his own children might now have resembled the two young people standing before him. Clarity and lucidity of utterance have replaced complexity and incoherence.

The effects created by the grammatical structures and the verse form are enhanced by the vocabulary and imagery of the two speeches. Leontes's descent from royalty of nature in Act I is emphasised by the almost colloquial tone of the speech, with its contractions, such as 'Ha' not you seen', 'say't, and justify't'; and its employment of offensive slang terminology such as 'slippery', 'hobby-horse', 'flax-wench' and the coarse verb 'puts to', meaning to have sex. Even when he veers into metaphor his insulting tone remains, as when he suggests that Camillo's 'eye-glass | Is thicker than a cuckold's horn'. His vocabulary shows him to be obsessed with illicit sexuality, emphasised again in his use of 'rank' as an adjective appropriate to Hermione's infidelity, employed in its common Shakespearean association of lust and physical corruption.

The impact of such vocabulary is frequently emphasised by assonance and alliteration, for example the long *u*s of 'rumour | Cannot be mute' and the short *a*s of 'as rank as

any flax-wench'; the hard *c*s of 'cuckold', 'cannot' and 'cogitation', the sibilants of 'slippery', 'confess, | or else', the *h*s of 'hobby-horse' and the reversed consonantal sequence of 'puts to [...] troth-plight'. These sounds enable the actor to emphasise contempt, disgust and sarcasm, the sound of the words supporting their meaning and associations.

Leontes's state of mind is emphasised too by the proliferation of negatives in his speech. As well as the word 'negative' itself, 'not' occurs three times, as does 'nor', with 'cannot' used once. Together with the central idea of inoperative senses, this language suggests that it is actually Leontes rather than Camillo who has lost the faculties of sight, hearing and 'cogitation', turning positive into negative.

The imagery of Leontes's speech in Act V could not be more different. Its keynote is a sense of spirituality, grace and health, though the language acknowledges also the 'infection' and 'sin' that have gone before. The religious language combines pagan and Christian terminology in its juxtaposition of 'the gods', 'the heavens' and 'heaven', and the opening invocation recalls the delicate climate and sweet air of Cleomenes and Dion's recollections of Delphos in III.1. If the gods are 'blessèd', Polixenes is 'holy', 'graceful' and 'sacred', and he too is 'blest' in having a son 'worthy his goodness'. The young couple, too, are 'goodly'. There is a lightness about the language of this passage, its aspirants and open vowel sounds creating a delicate softness, as in the phrase 'our air', effectively without consonants; the whispering sound of 'whilst'; the gentleness of 'here [...] have [...] holy'. These effects contrast with the hints of Leontes's lingering bitterness, evident in the antithetical alliterative balance of 'sacred' and 'sin', the ugliness of 'issueless' and the lost possibilities expressed in the repetition of 'might'.

So different are these two speeches that they might almost be spoken by different characters, and in a way they are. The Leontes of the final scenes is not the same Leontes as the jealous king of sixteen years before. And that, in a way, is one of the miracles of the play.

Further study

Editions of the play

All good editions of *The Winter's Tale* contain useful notes and stimulating introductions. Some of the best are listed below.

Innes, S. and Huddlestone, E. (eds) (1998) The Cambridge School Shakespeare, Cambridge University Press. This is the edition that has been used for the textual references in this Student Text Guide.

O'Connor, J. (ed.) (2003) New Longman Shakespeare, Longman.

Orgel, S. (ed.) (1996) The Oxford Shakespeare, Clarendon Press.

Pafford, J. H. P. (ed.) (1963) The Arden Shakespeare, 2nd series, Methuen.

Schanzer, E. (ed.) (1969) The New Penguin Shakespeare, Penguin.

Criticism of the play

Bartholomeusz, D. (1982) *'The Winter's Tale' in Performance in England and America, 1611–1976*, Cambridge University Press.

Draper, R. P. (1985) *The Winter's Tale*, Text and Performance Series, Macmillan.

Hardman, C. (1988) *The Winter's Tale*, Penguin Critical Studies, Penguin.

Hunt, M. (ed.) (1995) *'The Winter's Tale': Critical Essays*, Garland.

Innes, S. (2002) *The Winter's Tale*, Cambridge Student Guides, Cambridge University Press.

Muir, K. (ed.) (1969) *Shakespeare: 'The Winter's Tale'*, Casebook Series, Macmillan.

Nuttall, A. D. (1966) *The Winter's Tale*, Studies in English Literature, Edward Arnold.

Overton, B. (1989) *The Winter's Tale*, The Critics Debate, Macmillan.

Sanders, W. (1987) *The Winter's Tale*, Harvester New Critical Introductions to Shakespeare, Harvester Press.

Tatspaugh, P. E. (2002) *The Winter's Tale*, Shakespeare at Stratford, Arden Shakespeare.

Wood, L. and Wood, J. (1999) *The Winter's Tale*, York Notes Advanced, Longman.

Criticism of Shakespeare's last plays

All three of the books below, though dating from the middle of the twentieth century, are still well worth a look.

Tillyard, E. M. W. (1938) *Shakespeare's Last Plays*, Chatto and Windus.

Traversi, D. (1954) *Shakespeare: The Last Phase*, Hollis and Carter.

Wilson Knight, G. (1947) *The Crown of Life*, Oxford University Press (repr. Methuen, 1965).

Context

Bate, J. and Jackson, R. (eds) (1996) *Shakespeare: An Illustrated Stage History*, Oxford University Press.

Gurr, A. (1992) *The Shakespearean Stage 1574–1642* (3rd edn), Cambridge University Press.

Gurr, A. (1995) *William Shakespeare*, HarperCollins.

Gurr, A. (1996) *Playgoing in Shakespeare's London* (2nd edn), Cambridge University Press.

O'Connor, G. (1991) *William Shakespeare: A Life*, Hodder and Stoughton.

Parsons, K. and Mason, P. (eds) (1995) *Shakespeare in Performance*, Salamander Books.

Pritchard, R. E. (1998) *Shakespeare's England: Life in Elizabethan and Jacobean Times*, Sutton Publishing.

Russell Brown, J. (ed.) (1990) *Casebook: Studying Shakespeare*, Macmillan.

Wells, S. (1994) *Shakespeare: A Dramatic Life*, Sinclair-Stevenson.

Audiovisual resources and the internet

The Winter's Tale has not proved popular with film makers. The only production likely to be accessible from libraries and archives is Jane Howell's for the BBC Shakespeare series, first shown in 1981, with Anna Calder-Marshall and Jeremy Kemp.

Gregory Doran's 1999 Royal Shakespeare Company production, recorded at the Barbican Theatre in 2000, is available on Heritage Theatre DVD. Antony Sher and Alexandra Gilbreath play Leontes and Hermione. There is also a separate production casebook, with extracts from the production interspersed with a variety of interviews with the cast and production team. This is available on video as well as DVD.

Various audio versions of the play are available, including:
- Argo, featuring Margaretta Scott and William Squire
- Arkangel, featuring Sinead Cusack and Ciaran Hinds
- HarperCollins, featuring Peggy Ashcroft and John Gielgud

There is so much Shakespeare material available on the internet that it is difficult to know what is likely to be useful and reliable. The following are worth investigating:
- **http://shakespeare.palomar.edu** is entitled *Mr William Shakespeare and the Internet* and aims to be a complete, annotated scholarly guide to all the Shakespeare resources available online.
- **http://www.rsc.org.uk** is the Royal Shakespeare Company's website.
- **http://www.shakespeares-globe.org** is the official website of the reconstructed Globe Theatre.
- **http://www.shakespeare.org.uk** The Shakespeare Centre Library in Stratford-upon-Avon houses the archive of the Royal Shakespeare Company, where you can look up the records of all Stratford productions of *The Winter's Tale*, including prompt-books, photographs and press cuttings. Small groups or individual students can also arrange to watch videos of productions since the early 1980s. Recorded in performance with a fixed camera, the visual quality of these is sometimes poor, but they are useful records of how the play was staged and acted. Find out more via the website.